WRITINGS ON GRACE

BLAISE PASCAL

WRITINGS ON GRACE

THE COMPLETE *ÉCRITS SUR LA GRÂCE*

Translated with an Essay by

PAUL J. GRIFFITHS

THE CATHOLIC UNIVERSITY

OF AMERICA PRESS

Washington, D.C.

Ô qu'heureux sont ceux qui avec une liberté entière et une
pente invincible de leur volonté, et avec des charmes qui
les entraînent, aiment parfaitement et librement, et qui
sont obligés d'aimer nécessairement (Pascal, 'Prière pour
demander à Dieu le bon usage des maladies,' §5).

CONTENTS

PREFACE

Five years or so before he died in 1662, Blaise Pascal wrote fifteen inter-connected essays on grace which have collectively come to be known as the *Écrits sur la grâce*, or *Writings on Grace*. The *Writings* were not published before his death, and while they have appeared in French editions of his works since the eighteenth century, and have long been recognized as Pascal's most developed and idiosyncratic writing on grace, less than one-fifth of them has been published in English. This book provides a complete annotated translation of the *Writings*, together with an interpretive essay that clarifies their meaning and criticizes some of the positions Pascal takes in them.

The book has two principal purposes. The first is to provide a translation of the *Writings* sufficiently lucid, annotated, and explained to make them comprehensible to anglophone readers unschooled in the technicalities of seventeenth-century French theological writing. The second is to engage Pascal's characteristically uncompromising understanding of grace with sufficient argumentative vigor to encourage readers to engage it for themselves. Pascal was, to a remarkable degree, a polemical writer: his prose takes fire when it depicts his opponents' positions with clarity sufficient to persuade his readers to take pleasure in their destruction. We pay Pascal a compliment when we treat him likewise.

Serving these two purposes is more than enough for one book. Limiting myself to them has meant, however, paying no attention to many important questions about the *Writings*, including: the originality of Pascal's treatment of grace, whether within the broad context of the entire Christian tradition, the narrow one of his Port-Royal contemporaries, or any between; Pascal's accuracy or adequacy in handling and representing the sources he uses; the history of the reception and use of the *Writings*; the relations between them and other works by Pascal; and the orthodoxy of Pascal's grammar of grace, whether in his time or ours. These are topics for other books, and some of them have been addressed at length in what others have written about the *Writings*, a preliminary guide to which can be had from the notes and bibliography in this book.

Jean Mesnard, who died in 2016, devoted much thought to the *Writings* throughout his working life. Long ago he wrote that they are "une des clefs de toute l'oeuvre de Pascal."[1] He was right, and if this rendering of them into English permits anglophone readers of Pascal to see that he was, and which doors into Pascal's thought the key opens, it will have fulfilled its purpose.

---

1. Mesnard, *Pascal*, 105. This is a claim repeated by many other interpreters of Pascal. See, for example, Compagnon, ch. 21.

At various times during the last fifteen years of his life, Blaise Pascal (1623–1662) wrote about grace. This was a vehemently controversial topic among Catholics in the France of the 1650s, as it had been for most of the century prior; arguments about it generated a substantial literature during the seventeenth century. Some of this writing was occasioned by the Reformation. As French Catholic theologians became aware of the ways in which grace had been theorized by Calvin and Luther, among others, they developed elaborate refutations. But more was occasioned by intra-Catholic disputes, particularly among Molinists, Dominicans, Jesuits, and Augustinians. By the early seventeenth century, intra-Catholic arguments about the varieties and purposes of grace had reached such density and intractability that Pope Paul V called a moratorium on some aspects of the question. This did not prevent further writing about the topic however. Fresh arguments were prompted by the posthumous publication of Cornelius Jansenius's *Augustinus* in 1640 and the papal condemnations of that work by Innocent X in 1653 and Alexander VII in 1656. As a result, by the 1650s debates about grace reached a new depth and scope in France.

Such arguments were one of the focal points around which the theology of Port-Royal developed, and it is therefore not surprising that Pascal should have written about the topic.

He did that most publicly and fluently in the *Lettres Provinciales*, published under the name Louis de Montalte between January 1656 and May 1657. Several of those letters are devoted entirely to grace. There are also remarks on the topic preserved in the collection posthumously handed down under the title *Pensées*. But Pascal's most precise, technical, and developed writing about grace is in neither of those places, but rather in the short documents that have come to be known collectively as the *Écrits sur la grâce*, or *Writings on Grace*. It is not clear exactly when these writings were composed, but it was probably in the second half of the 1650s, possibly later than the *Lettres Provinciales*, and very likely not all at one time. These writings were not titled, completed, published, or widely shared during Pascal's life. They were, according to written testimony of his nephew, Louis Périer, found after his death among Pascal's manuscripts in the form of a single volume, which *"contient plusieurs pièces imparfaites sur la grâce et le Concile de Trente."*[1] Some of the pages were written in Pascal's own hand and some in that of a copyist.

That manuscript volume has not survived, but copies were made, and one of them, made not long after Pascal's death, is extant. This manuscript contains the first fourteen of the fifteen short documents that comprise the *Writings* and is the principal basis of all printed editions. The only witness to the text of the *Writings* independent of that manuscript was another manuscript that Louis Périer had made at a date now impossible to determine precisely. It included §7 and §15 among other material, and was very likely made directly from the original, partially autograph volume. That manuscript also has not survived, (or at least is no longer locatable), but the tradition stemming from it informed printed editions and summaries of the *Writings* made from the eighteenth to the twentieth century. Together with the traces in printed editions of the lost minor one, the surviving major manuscript, then, is as close as we can come to the now lost volume containing the *Writings* deposited by Louis Périer in the library of Saint-Germain-des-Prés in 1711.[2]

The two most important and widely used editions of the *Writings* are those by Jean Mesnard and Michel Le Guern. Mesnard's was published in 1991 in the third volume of his projected edition of Pascal's

---

1. Périer's testimony is quoted in full in Le Guern, *Oeuvres*, 2:1210.

2. For these details about provenance and transmission, I rely principally upon Lafuma, *Deux pièces*; Mesnard, *Oeuvres*, 3:487–511; and Le Guern, *Oeuvres*, 2:1210–16. Cantillon's "Comment donc écrire?" is salutary about the manuscript tradition and its significance. The principal surviving manuscript witness to the *Writings* is *Bibliothèque Nationale, fonds française* 12249, *folios* 615–788. I have not consulted that or any other manuscript.

works; (Mesnard died in 2016 without completing the project). Le Guern's was published in 2000 in the second volume of his two-volume edition of Pascal's works. These editions represent opposed editorial philosophies, and although the manuscript evidence is the same for each and the words contained in each are almost the same, the order in which the material is presented is drastically different.

Mesnard draws upon clear indications from within the manuscripts' fifteen documents that different parts of the whole work belong to different genres, (letter, treatise, florilegium, doxography, and so on). He reconstitutes the whole to bring together the elements that belong to each genre, then orders the newly constituted parts perspicuously. This makes the trajectory of argument of the whole work clearer than it is in the order given to the material in the manuscripts. And, it may more closely approach what Pascal would have done had he brought the work to completion. Mesnard's *Writings* begins with a letter, segues into a discourse, and ends with a treatise. Those three parts are then further, and minutely, subdivided.

Le Guern, in part reacting against Mesnard, follows the order in which the material is given in the manuscripts. That approach yields the division of the *Writings* into fifteen short documents; the shortest a few hundred words long, and the longest rather more than five thousand. Le Guern acknowledges what is indisputable. The *Writings,* as they stand in the manuscripts, lack a polished form and are replete with stutters, recapitulations, repetitions, experiments with different genres, evidence of second and third thoughts, and so on. He acknowledges, too, that had Pascal worked more on the *Writings,* it is likely, or at least possible, that many of these difficulties would have been cleared up and smoothed away. But his editorial goal is to present the material as closely as possible to the order in which Pascal left it, and he thinks that the manuscripts likely provide closer witness to that than do later editorial imaginings. His edition betrays no interest in speculating, counterfactually, about what Pascal might have done had he worked more on the *Writings.*

Both editors have precursors. The enterprise of reordering the manuscript material for a printed edition began in the eighteenth century, and that of following the manuscripts as closely as possible only a little later. The two enterprises are incommensurable in the sense that each is coherent and informed by assumptions and purposes the validity of which cannot be addressed from a neutral perspective. If you have Mesnard's assumptions and goals (and his indefatigable energy), you will produce an edition of the *Writings* like his. If you have Le Guern's, you will end up with something like his.

The two sets of assumptions and purposes, however, yield profoundly different works. To read Mesnard's and Le Guern's editions successively is to read two works whose words are almost the same, but whose feel and form are utterly different. It is as if one were to read Wittgenstein's *Philosophische Untersuchungen* as printed in the 2009 bilingual edition, and then to read it reordered according to some editor's understanding of which remarks fit more perspicuously with which. Or, as if one were to read the brief chapters of Machado de Assis's *Memórias Póstuma de Brás Cubas* in the order in which they appeared in their first magazine publication, and then read them reordered according to the chronological sequence of events mentioned within the text. Work on the *Writings*, then, requires a choice: which edition should one read and work on?

I have chosen to read and work on Le Guern's edition. There are two reasons. The first, and less important, is that the text as presented there is easier to read than what Mesnard provides. His pages are sufficiently cluttered with editorial matter that they approach illegibility. The second, and more important, is that the order given the material in Le Guern's edition is more appropriate to the topic than Mesnard's. Grace is, for Christians, hard to think about. It was in the seventeenth century as it still is, among the knottiest topics in Christian theology. Writing about it ought not yield smoothness, whether in structure or style. The stammer, the second thought, the self-check, the retracing, the repetition of an earlier thought in a moderately different key—all these are evident in Le Guern's presentation of Pascal's text. They show a pen at work, not an artifact reconstructed for specious perspicuity. My translation does the same.[3]

---

3. This decision to use Le Guern rather than Mesnard does not indicate that I take Le Guern's edition to be closer to the mind of Pascal than Mesnard's, or the reverse. I have no interest in the mind of Pascal, only in some words on paper under his name.

Given this decision, what, in brief outline, is the form and content of the *Writings*?

The first begins in the form of a letter to an unnamed addressee. Its writer says that he is responding to a request for clarification about the Council of Trent's claim that observance of the commandments is possible for those who have been rectified—set right by baptism. The letter form soon drops away. But the interwoven topics of what it means for some course of action to be possible for the baptized, or for anyone at all, and of how the texts of Trent should be understood on that question, are treated in various ways throughout the first five *Writings*. The movement of the prose is far from linear. The text of Trent is taken up closely, then dropped, then returned to. Technical grammatical and philosophical distinctions about possibility and ability (What are the conditions that make it reasonable to say that some action is possible for us? Do they differ from the conditions that make it reasonable to say that we are able to do something?) are undertaken, dropped, and returned to. And there are several attempts to relate both these discussions, about Trent and about the logic and grammar of possibility and ability, to controversies about Pelagianism from the fifth and sixth centuries. Pascal cites, quotes, and discusses patristic writers on those topics, with most of his attention given to Augustine. His interest in doing this is to suggest that his precise technical understanding of what Christians need from God in order to be able to do anything good, such as observe the commandments, is identical with and supported by Augustine and other anti-Pelagian writers. And so, by extension, Pascal suggests that the position argued in the *Writings* is the same as the Catholic position, and, therefore, true.

Beginning in the sixth *Writing*, about one-third of the way through the whole, the terrain shifts. The possibility-ability-power-grace questions (and the questions about Trent) do not go away, but they begin to open out into others. Among these are whether God provides the helps necessary to good action to all or only to some among the rectified, and if only to some, why, and under what conditions? These are questions about election, perseverance, predestination, certitude, and gift.

I have, of course, benefited enormously from Mesnard's work on matters such as Pascal's sources. Gratitude is the only possible response to that work.

As the sixth *Writing* progresses, they begin to displace the first set of questions—or, perhaps better, to show where that first set of questions leads and what it presupposes. The letter form resurfaces here, as well: there is an unnamed interlocutor (the same one?), and Pascal is often in hortatory mood.

The seventh *Writing* opens with the most abstract and formal attempt so far in the work to provide a lexicon and syntax for thinking and writing about the relation between God's agency and ours—about what grace is and what it does, and about who gets grace and who does not, and why. It culminates with the first doxographic sketch in the work, which is to say a map of the territory of thought about these questions, and an allotment of each position to named parties—Calvinists, Molinists, Augustinians.

With the eighth *Writing*, a new set of terms is introduced: there is a distinction between two desertions (ours of God, and God's of us). That distinction permits analysis of who leaves whom and in what order. Is damnation—living irretrievably, unfailingly, endlessly, horizonlessly, in the absence of God—a result of what we have done and are doing, or a result of what God has done and is doing? Pascal shows that, and how, both can be said, and his treatment of that involves a depiction of what the sin-dazed condition we are in means for grace. Grace can only be effective if it outdoes the bedazzlements of sin by supplying a more intense delight in God than evil does in sin. The running contrast is between Adam's situation before the Fall and ours after it.

Then, in the ninth *Writing*, the doxographic analysis of positions on sin and grace, coupled with the drama of the double desertion, is turned back toward and woven together with the topic of possibility and ability already treated in the first five *Writings*. An account of what we can do with the help of grace and cannot do without its help is, by the end of the ninth *Writing*, bound up with and shown to be inseparable from an account of God's inscrutable choices and purposes evident in the double desertion. Increasingly heavy patristic guns are brought forward, so that by the end of the ninth *Writing*, Pascal has begun to provide a dossier, a florilegium, of weighty texts from such as Augustine, Prosper of Aquitaine, and Fulgentius of Ruspe, in support of the grammar of grace he advocates. This continues in the tenth

Écrit, which, returning to the letter-form, largely treats the possibility-ability-capacity-perseverance questions raised already, but now with the help of accumulating authorities. Pascal's words begin to be outnumbered by those of the authorities he quotes.

With the eleventh *Writing*, there is a sudden and dramatic tonal shift. Pascal becomes poetical, beautifully so, as he sketches the regress of humans from Adam to ourselves, and the place and workings of grace in that regress. The first half of this *Writing* is, as I read it, the most characteristically Pascalian in style of the *Writings*, and the most delightful to read. Following that sketch, he returns to doxography, and contrasts the Augustinian view of the state of innocence and its loss, which is also his, and, as he depicts it, the only possible one for Catholics, with that of Calvinists and Pelagians, who, as they appear in his words hold contrary positions on the Fall and what follows it, between which the Augustinian view finds a middle.[4]

The twelfth *Writing* turns back to the double desertion discussed in the eighth and ninth, and treats that topic now as an instance of, and within the frame of, an analysis of apparent contradictions in Scripture and the writings of Augustine. The analysis is partly logical. To say, for instance, that we both do and do not desert God before God deserts us, may be contradictory in appearance. But if the term of art, *délaissement* (desertion), has a double meaning—Pascal likes to call it "equivocal," a word he has already used for analysis of the Council of Trent's texts on these matters in the first *Writing*—then the apparent contradiction can easily be resolved by discriminating the meanings. But the analysis is also substantive. It shows that the double sense of terms such as *desertion* and *ability* requires showing something of substance about the relation between humans and God. This, too, is evident in the twelfth *Writing*.

The thirteenth and fourteenth *Writings* are florilegia, mostly of excerpts from patristic works, but with a few from magisterial and medieval works. These two *Writings* contain almost none of Pascal's words. They are materials for arguments and demonstrations given in the first

---

4. Pascal has little interest in actual Calvinists or once-actual Pelagians; he uses them, as he also does Molina and Molinists, and Luther and Lutherans, as ideal types, counters in the game of truth.

twelve, and many of them are deployed (quoted, alluded to, and so on), elsewhere in the *Writings*, especially in the second, sixth, and ninth. The excerpts assembled in the thirteenth are given in French, without any explicit identification of source; those in the fourteenth are given in Latin, with brief notations of source. There is no overlap between the two collections of excerpts. A remarkable feature of the French florilegium in the thirteenth is that its central thread is delight (*délectation* and cognate words). It is almost as though Pascal had read through his sources (rather, source: Pascal draws all his excerpts in the thirteenth from a single anthology published by Jean Sinnich in 1648) pen in hand, underlining delight words and then including what he found. There are twenty-three excerpts in the thirteenth, eighteen of which are explicit in their treatment of delight. The remaining five do not contain delight words but are nevertheless in service to the same theme. The fourteenth contains twenty-seven excerpts which are threaded around the vocabulary of delight to almost the same extent as those in the thirteenth.

The *Writings* conclude with a fifteenth document, in which the differences between Calvinists and Molinists on the workings of grace in salvation and damnation are reprised (they were already stated in the seventh and eighth *Writings*) and connected with medieval and then-recent (sixteenth- and seventeenth-century) analyses of these matters by theological faculties in Louvain, Douai, and Paris. The central point here is to underscore the claim that the Augustinian view of grace and associated topics, set out and defended throughout the *Writings*, is also the view of the orthodox tradition from the beginning of Christianity until the seventeenth century.

Pascal's two axiomatic commitments in the *Writings* are: that all good action requires particular graces; and that these required graces are not given to all. The controversial questions to which he applies these axioms have to do, first, with the relations between possibility and ability in the sphere of human action; and second, with the effects of the Fall upon the need for graces. He uses his axioms as a means, positively, to sketch what he takes to be the right position on these controversial topics, and, negatively, to identify the principal errors that can be and have been made with respect to them. Pascal proceeds, almost exclusively, in polemical mode. He identifies errors and shows what he takes to be the correct position by engaging and refuting them. The polemic has two foci: one is the interpretation of authoritative texts, mostly conciliar and patristic; and the other is conceptual and grammatical, treating coherence and adequacy to ordinary usage. There is also, as a thread running through almost the entirety of the *Writings*, present in all but the thirteenth and fourteenth, a doxographic concern. Pascal maps the conceptual territory by elucidating the principal positions on his controversial concerns, and allotting them to schools of thought—namely, Lutheran, Calvinist, Molinist, Manichean, Pelagian, and Augustinian—with the Augustinian positions presented as both true and orthodox. A typical flourish is: "the Manichees were the Lutherans of their time as the Lutherans are the Manichees of ours" (§2).

All that—the axioms, the polemic, the conceptual-grammatical demonstrations, the interpretations of texts—is presented as a series of sketches, brief illuminations from different angles of a landscape overgrown with word-tangles. Trent's texts appear again and again as one of those tangles. Augustine's anti-Manichaean and anti-Pelagian writings are another. Various and incompatible ways of depicting the Fall and its effects are a third. Pascal's sketches prune the tangles, trimming back suckers and wayward shoots so that the plant can grow straight toward the sun. (The treatment of the word *toujours* in the first and second *Writings*, most especially in the opening movement of the second, is a pellucid and paradigmatic instance of the pruning shears at work. Similar are the treatments of *monde, tous, plusieurs*, and *peu* in the eleventh *Writing*.) The sketches do this work in fits and starts, and the upshot is that the *Writings* read as a series of pencil-sketches of a single landscape, made by the artist in different lights and from different angles. There is no single, definitive final picture, but the various sketches, taken together, show a habitable landscape.[5]

Pascal is, in my judgment, entirely and importantly correct in his view that sequestering any aspect of good human action from the need

5. In describing the *Writings* like this, I borrow from Wittgenstein's description of the form of his *Philosophische Untersuchungen* in the foreword to that work (3–4). His remarks are, he writes, *Landschaftskizzen*. The image applies also, and perhaps better, to the *Writings*.

for grace is damaging to the entire fabric of Christian thought and practice. He is also, so far as I can see, fundamentally wrong in his view that the graces required for good action are not offered to all, and in the conclusions that flow from such a view. I write more about the reasons for thinking him right and wrong in these ways in the interpretive essay that follows the translation. That he is not always right (no one is always right) does not in the least vitiate the value of Pascal's work. His mapping of the territory, and the stuttering vigor with which the map is filled in, may, if read closely and slowly, clarify some turbid and muddied waters.

The translation of the *Writings* that follows is made from the text given in the second volume of Michel Le Guern's edition of Pascal's works. I have also throughout consulted Jean Mesnard's text of the *Writings* in the third volume of his edition of Pascal's works.[1] I follow Le Guern's text closely.

In particular, I reproduce the expressive features of Le Guern's text, namely: its paragraphing, which is heavier than feels natural in current English; its sentence division, which also differs from what comes naturally to an anglophone; its italicizations, which often indicate quotations or approximate quotations, sometimes the mention of a word or phrase rather than its use, and sometimes emphasis; its quotation marks (« … », here represented with "…"); and its parentheses.

I diverge from Le Guern's text in the following ways, which I do not note as they occur. I omit the brackets ([ ]) he uses to indicate blank space in the manuscripts; and I sometimes provide a noun where Le Guern's text has a pronoun, and, more rarely, a pronoun where it has a noun. Otherwise, Le Guern's text is what I translate, and I have tried to write English close in rhythm and register to the French in Le Guern's edition.

The only published English versions of any parts of the *Writings* longer than a sentence or two known to me are: Jan Miel's of a dozen or so excerpts from several of them; A. J. Krailsheimer's of a dozen or so sentences from the seventh; and Honor Levi's of most of the first and all the eleventh.[2] Together these account for less than one-fifth of

---

1. Le Guern, *Oeuvres*, 2:211–316; Mesnard, *Oeuvres*, 3:642–799. See also Lafuma, *Oeuvres*, 310–48.

2. Miel, 202–11; Krailsheimer, 27–29; Levi & Levi, 205–26.

the whole. I draw gratefully upon the work these translators have done.

Most of the *Writings* are in French, but there is also some material in Latin, and that provides particular difficulties. In the body of my translation, I leave in Latin what appears in that language in Le Guern's edition. But I fully translate into English, in the notes, any Latin that appears in the text, unless Pascal's French (and therefore also my English) immediately translates, glosses, or comments upon it in such a way as to make a translation otiose.

There are particular issues connected with the dossier of Latin excerpts given in the fourteenth *Writing*. Pascal renders some of these excerpts into French elsewhere, particularly in the second, and paraphrases, refers to, or summarizes others in other places. In spite of this, I provide, in the notes to the fourteenth, a full English rendering of each Latin excerpt given there. I do this partly for the convenience of readers, but partly also because Pascal often translates freely—sometimes so much so that it is hard to say whether what he does is translating rather than summarizing, paraphrasing, distilling, or riffing. It may be useful for readers to see what a more literal rendering of the Latin looks like, and to compare the English of an excerpt made directly from Latin with that of the same excerpt made via Pascal's French.

Pascal's freedom in rendering his excerpts, and his proclivity for deploying the same excerpt more than once in the *Writings*, results in the same original appearing differently in French (and therefore also in English) in different places in the *Writings*. I do not comment on these differences in the notes. Anglophone readers should note that variations in the rendering of a single excerpt are due to Pascal rather than to me.

A representative example is Pascal's deployment of an excerpt from Prosper of Aquitaine's *Ad capitula objectionum Vincentianarum responsiones*. He uses this five times in the *Writings*: in §1, §8, twice in §9, and in §12. The variations in the French he provides, (he does not give the Latin), are minor, but sometimes significant and always interesting:

- Dieu ne quitte point, s'il n'est quitté. (§1)
- Dieu ne quitte point, si l'on ne le quitte; et il fait bien souvent qu'on ne le quitte point < ... > Mais d'où vient qu'il retient ceux-ci, et non pas ceux-là? Il n'est ni permis de le rechercher, ni possible de le trouver. (§8)

• Que Dieu ne quitte point le juste s'il ne le quitte le premier <…>
Que Dieu quitte le premier le juste. (§9)

• Dieu ne quitte point un juste, si le juste ne le quitte auparavant
<…> Et bien souvent il fait qu'il ne le quitte point. <…> Pourquoi
Dieu retient ceux-ci et non pas ceux-là est une chose qui est défendue
d'être recherchée et qu'il est impossible de trouver. (§9)

• Dieu ne quitte point si l'on ne le quitte, et il fait bien souvent qu'on
ne le quitte point. Mais d'où vient qu'il retient ceux-ci, et qu'il ne retient
pas ceux-la? Il n'est ni permis de le chercher, ni possible de le trouver.
(§12)

Perhaps Pascal is glancing at the Latin original each time as he provides his French. Perhaps he is recalling, or half-recalling, the words or
the gravamen of the excerpt. Whatever the case, he did not reconcile
his renderings with one another, and a rendering into English of the
French he provides ought not do so either.

I have not tried to find one-to-one English equivalents for all Pascal's
terms for art. I have, however, made some decisions that yield transparency, in the sense that whenever a particular English word appears
in the translation, it represents the same French word. (This is not to
say that whenever that French word appears it is rendered by the same
English word—the transparency is one-way). I have also sometimes
used a single English word consistently to render two or more French
ones in ways that might be useful for readers to keep in mind. And there
are some instances in which my choices are against the stream. I provide
brief discussion of these matters in the glossary, immediately below.

The notes to the translation are intended to identify Pascal's quotations and allusions, and to explain points about the translation that
would remain puzzling without elucidation. In the *Writings*, Pascal
quotes and otherwise draws from many sources. Sometimes he identifies them, but much more often not. Mostly, his quotations, summaries, and references come not directly from the works he is quoting,
summarizing, or referring to, but rather from secondary sources of his
own time—anthologies, florilegia, digests, and historical or polemical
works. In my identifications of his sources, I provide, where relevant,
references both to the primary source Pascal treats and to the secondary source from which he took it. My identifications in the notes of

premodern sources used by Pascal, and of locations within them for his quotations and summaries, sometimes differ from his (when he provides them). That is because editorial work on the premodern works he uses has advanced considerably since the seventeenth century. This has led, inter alia, to differences in systems of reference. My goal in identifying locations within premodern works for Pascal's quotations and other uses is to provide information sufficient for twenty-first-century readers to find Pascal's premodern sources, should they wish to.

In the notes, reference to the *Writings* is by section number (§), and to all other works by author alone (when there is only one work by that author in the bibliography), author with short title (when there is more than one work by that author in the bibliography), or short title alone (when the work is listed by title in the bibliography). There is an entry in the bibliography for every work mentioned in the notes.

The *Writings* are saturated in Scripture, as are the sources they use. In the *Writings,* Pascal rarely locates his quotations from or allusions to Scripture by naming the scriptural book from which they come, (the sources he quotes and alludes to occasionally do, and when they do, he usually follows them). He does sometimes indicate author or speaker (Jesus, Paul, David, and so on). My locations of scriptural quotations and allusions in the notes follow the chapter- and verse-divisions of the *Nova Vulgata* in the *editio typica altera* of 1986. Consulting this, or any other twentieth- or twenty-first-century scriptural translation made from Hebrew and Greek, will often yield text different from that given here. That is sometimes because Pascal relies upon the text of the Vulgate, which often differs from the Hebrew and Greek texts established and relied upon by translators of our time, and not infrequently from the text of the *Nova Vulgata* as well. Sometimes, this is because Pascal is alluding to, paraphrasing, echoing, or summarizing Scripture rather than quoting it directly. Pascal, in referring to Scripture, sometimes seems to be rendering the Latin of the Vulgate directly, sometimes to be relying upon the French in *La Sainte Bible contenant le Vieil et Nouveau Testament, traduit en française selon la vulgaire édition latine* (Rouen, 1648), and sometimes to be supplying scriptural texts or echoes of them from memory, whether of Latin or French. I have in all cases rendered the French Pascal gives.

GLOSSARY

ability/to be able to—transparent to *pouvoir*, noun and verb; terms of art, extensively discussed and deployed throughout; they connote, most generally, our capacity to do something; see *power*.

to accomplish—transparent to *accomplir*; indicating, usually, the relation those who persevere in righteousness have to the commandments, and by extension to the Christian life.

balance—transparent to *indifférence*; a condition of equilibrium between two alternatives in which each is possible and there is equal inclination toward each; see *unobstructed/unobstructedly*.

choice/to choose—indifferently for *arbitre/arbitrer* and *choix/choisir*; particularly in the phrases *libre arbitre* or *liberum arbitre*, both of which I render *free choice* or *freedom of choice*; see *will/to will*.

to concur—transparent to *concourir*; what God's will and ours and God's action and ours do with respect to one another; see *will/to will*; *choice/to choose*

delight/to delight—transparent to *délectation(délice)/délecter*; a response we may have to both evil and God; what God gives to us to make us able to live well.

desertion—transparent to *délaissement*; ours of God and God's of us; the dialectic of damnation; see *to leave*.

effective grace—transparent to *grâce efficace*; a grace that guarantees perseverance in the Christian life for as long as it is given; synonymous with *effective help*; see: *sufficient grace; sufficient help*.

effective help—transparent to *secours efficace*; help that guarantees perseverance in the Christian life for as long as given; synonymous with *effective grace*.

help/to help—indifferently for *secours/secourir* and *aide/aider*; indicating a particular relation God bears to us, which comes in kinds; see: *effective grace; effective help*.

to keep—indifferently for *garder* and *observer*; indicating, usually, the relation the righteous may have to the commandments, namely that of living according to them for a while.

to leave—indifferently for *laisser, quitter,* and *abandonner*: something we can do to God, and that God can do to us; see *desertion.*

love—indifferently for *amour* and *charité*; something we need from God that God sometimes supplies; something we are sometimes able to return to God.

power—transparent to *puissance*; close to *ability.*

righteous/rectified/righteousness—transparent to *juste/justifié/justice* (and, in Latin, to *justus/justificatus/justice*); *righteous* is a label for those who have been *rectified* from their previous servitude to sin, typically by baptism, and who therefore participate in *righteousness* for as long as given *effective grace* to do so.

sufficient grace—transparent to *grâce suffisante*: grace that provides help enough to make right action possible, but that does not guarantee such action; see: *effective grace; effective help; sufficient help.*

sufficient help—transparent to *secours suffisant*: help enough to make right action possible, but not to guarantee it; see: *effective grace; effective help; sufficient grace.*

unobstructed/unobstructedly—transparent to *prochain/prochainement*; if *x* is unobstructed with respect to *y*, or acts unobstructedly with respect to *y*, then nothing stands between *x*, or *x*'s action, and *y*; to have unobstructed ability with respect to some action is to be able at once to do it without external help; all unobstructed abilities are alone sufficient to bring about their objects; see *ability/ able to,* together with which these words most often occur in the *Writings.*

to use, or *to make use of*—transparent to *se servir*; denotes most commonly the relation between free choice and unobstructed ability; this relation is lacking for all humans *post lapsum,* but was present for Adam.

will/to will—transparent to *volonté/vouloir*; both God and we have this and do this; see *choice/to choose*; and *to concur.*

WRITINGS ON GRACE

§1[1]

―――

I lack leisure, books, and capacity to respond to you just as I would like; nevertheless, I will do what I can here, so that when you see in writing the things I have often said to you, they will make more of an impression, and you will not need me to repeat them to you.

You ask me to respond to these words from the eleventh chapter of the sixth session of the Council of Trent: *the commandments are not impossible for the righteous*. I will do what I can.

The proposition, *the commandments are possible for the righteous*, has two quite different senses, each distant from the other. This is not a scholastic distinction; it is solid and real, both in the nature of the topic and in the terms the Council uses.

The first sense that offers itself, which you believe to be that of the Council but which you will find not to be so, is that the righteous, considered at any moment of their righteousness, are always unobstruct edly able to accomplish the commandments in the next moment; that

---

1. I translate §1 from Le Guern, *Oeuvres*, 2:211–20; see also Mesnard, *Oeuvres*, 3:648–62. An English version of about eighty percent of §1 is in Levi & Levi, 205–12. Throughout §1, Pascal appeals to, quotes, echoes, and discusses the Council of Trent's Decree on Rectification, together with its associated canons. He consulted the Latin text of that decree and its canons in Chifflet, 24–49. In §1, he quotes only from the eleventh and thirteenth chapters of the Decree, and from the eighteenth, twenty-second, and twenty-fifth canons. Underlined sentences or phrases in §1 otherwise unidentified by me are quotations or near-quotations from those chapters and those canons. Pascal's formulations, *the commandments are possible for the righteous*, and *the commandments are not impossible for the righteous*, are not direct quotations but, rather, something like distillations of the chapter and the canons—representations, perhaps, of what he takes to be their essential conceptual content. He takes the two formulations to be equivalent.

1

is the view of the remainder of the Pelagians,[2] which the Church has always fought against, and particularly at this Council.

The second sense, which does not offer itself so immediately but which is nevertheless that of the Council, is that the righteous, acting as such and by a movement of love, are able to accomplish the commandments when they act out of love. I understand very well that there is so little room for doubt that actions done out of love conform to the precepts, that it is difficult to believe that the Council wanted to define something so clear; but when you consider that the Lutherans formally hold that the actions of the righteous, even those done out of love, are necessarily always sinful, and that concupiscence, which always rules in this life, ruins the effect of love so much that however righteous we may be, and by whatever movements of love we might act, covetous desire always plays such a part that not only do we fail to accomplish the precepts, but we violate them, and that we are therefore absolutely incapable of keeping them no matter what grace helps us—then you will be sure that the Council had to rule against such an insupportable error.

You see how much the two senses differ: according to the one, it is clear that the righteous are able to persevere in righteousness; according to the other, it is clear that the commandments are possible for love to the extent that love is with the righteous in this life; and although the two senses have been expressed here in quite different words, they may both be expressed in these words: *the commandments are possible for the righteous.*

Because this proposition is equivocal, you ought not find it strange that it is possible to agree with it in one sense and deny it in the other. Also, each sense has had its opposing heretics.

The remainder of the Pelagians hold that the commandments are always possible for the righteous in the first sense, while the Church denies it.

The Lutherans hold that the commandments are impossible in the second sense; the Church denies it.

---

2. This phrase, *les restes des Pélagiens,* appears to be derived from Prosper of Aquitaine's letter to Augustine of 428 or 429, where Prosper uses it to designate the priests of Marseilles who follow John Cassian's thought on grace and human agency. It is effectively interchangeable with *semi-pélagians*, which Pascal also uses.

So the Council, needing to combat two errors so different (for it is as heretical to hold that the commandments are always possible in the first sense as to hold that they are impossible in the second) that they are entirely distinct, refutes them separately. It combats Luther's error in the eleventh chapter, which is directed only at that heresiarch, as well as in canons eighteen and twenty-five, which formulate it; and it opposes the error of the semi-Pelagians in the thirteenth chapter, as well as in canons sixteen and twenty-two, which formulate it. Accordingly, its object in the eleventh chapter is only to show that the righteous, acting by the love of God, are able to act without sin, and that they are able to keep the commandments if they act by love; it is not to show that the righteous are always unobstructedly able to retain the love which makes the commandments possible.

The Council's object in the thirteenth chapter is to declare it false that the righteous are always unobstructedly able to persevere, anathematizing in the formulation of canon twenty-two those who say that the righteous are able to persevere in righteousness without special help, and consequently affirming that such help is not shared by all the righteous.

In this, the Council establishes that the righteous not only lack actual perseverance without special help, but that they also lack the ability to persevere without special help; which is exactly to say that all the righteous who lack this special ability are also unable to accomplish the commandments in the next moment, because perseverance is nothing other than accomplishing the commandments in the next moments; nonetheless, the Council's determination does not contradict that of the eleventh chapter, that *the commandments are not impossible for the righteous,* because of the different senses of the proposition.

To prove what I say, it is necessary only to translate all of the eleventh chapter; if you have that done, you will see the sense of the Council open up. The Council declares first its proposition, *the commandments are not impossible for the righteous,* which are St. Augustine's words.[3] And to examine in what sense he intends the proposition, I ask you

3. Early in the eleventh chapter of Trent's Decree on Rectification, there are echoes, though not quite verbatim ones, of Augustine's *De natura* 43.50 (also in §14). Those may be what Pascal points to here; they are indicated in the marginal notes of Chifflet, 34.

only to look at the proof the Council provides of it, the conclusion it derives from its proof, and the canons that formulate it. For if the proof it gives applies only to the proposition's first sense, if the conclusion it draws applies univocally only to that same first sense, and if even the canons are purely about that first sense, who can doubt that the proposition has that first sense?

Here is the proof: the commandments are not impossible for the righteous *because those who are God's children*, which is to say the righteous, *love Jesus Christ, and he has said that those who love him keep his word*,[4] which is to say his precepts. This proof is excellent for showing possibility in the first sense, which is to say for showing that the commandments are possible for love; for Jesus Christ has said that those who love him keep his commandments. But the proof is valueless for showing possibility in the other sense, which is to say for the future; for it is well said that those who love Jesus Christ in the present keep his commandments when they love him in that same present; but not that they will be able to keep them in the future. Also, the Council indicates in the same place, *the righteous are able to keep the commandments with God's help*.

And then, having cited many passages from Scripture that command righteousness and keeping the precepts, which would be ridiculous if human nature, even aided by grace, were entirely incapable of doing those things, the Council concludes in this way: *from which it is certain that those who say the righteous sin in all their good actions oppose the true faith*.

Consequently, the Council claims to have proved its proposition that *the commandments are not impossible for the righteous*, when by means of its proof *that those who love Jesus Christ keep his word* it draws the conclusion that *therefore the righteous do not sin in all their good actions*—is it possible, then, to deny that the Council has claimed nothing different in its equivocal proposition than what it says in its conclusion, which can be taken in no different sense, that is: *the righteous do not sin when they act well by the movement of grace?*[5]

And this is perfectly clarified by the canons formulated about this,

---

4. John 14:23, alluded to in the text of Trent.

5. That Pascal uses *grâce* here shows that he treats it as sometimes exchangeable with *amor/charité*.

which are always the substance, as it were, the soul of the chapters. Here are all the canons the Council provides about this possibility:

Canon twenty-five: *Any who say that the righteous sin venially in every good work, or, what is still more insupportable, that they sin mortally, and that they thereby deserve eternal punishment and are not damned as a result only because God does not impute their works to them for damnation, are to be anathematized.*

Is not the sense of the Council clear?

Canon eighteen: *Any who say that keeping the commandments is impossible for all, even when rectified and established in grace, are to be anathematized.*

Is there anything more clear? It seems that the Council feared that its formulation might be misinterpreted, and therefore, was not content to say, *any who say that the commandments are impossible for the righteous, are to be anathematized*; instead it says, *any who say that the commandments are impossible for the righteous established in grace are to be anathematized*; the result is that it is impossible to believe that the Council spoke of that Pelagian possibility. It clearly appears that by using these terms it combats only those who say that the commandments are impossible for the righteous even with grace, and at the time when they are established in grace, to use those terms; for in view of the fact that the canons are always designed to be very concise and constrained, the Council would have added *established in grace* to *rectified* only to make its intention clearer and its sense unequivocal.[6]

I leave it to you to judge how weak those are who search this chapter of the Council for equivocation. Although this would suffice for a reply to what you have asked of me, I nevertheless add another proof to satisfy you more fully. The words, *the commandments are not impossible for the righteous*, are taken from St. Augustine, who is cited in the margins of the Council;[7] it is not that these words are used by the Council

6. In this paragraph and the one preceding it, Pascal shifts back and forth between *juste* (righteous) and *justifié* (rectified), even in what seem to be quotations from the eighteenth canon. These shifts are reflected in my English. The canon itself, in Latin, uses *justificatus*, for which Pascal, in his rendering of the entire canon, above, uses *juste*. But in this sentence, in the course of discussing the canon's verbal form, he uses *justifié*, whence *rectified*. See the glossary for further discussion.

7. Augustine, *De natura* 69.83 (also in §§9, 10, 14, 15), is cited in the margin of

in a sense contrary to St. Augustine's; rather, the Council deploys these words only for their sense—to do anything else would have been to act in bad faith.

To see clearly that whenever St. Augustine used these words he intended nothing other than what the Council does with them, it is necessary only to look at his works. I believe that he almost never uses them without explaining them in this way: that the commandments are not impossible with love and are impossible without it; and that the only reason the commandments are given is to make us understand the need we have to receive this love from God. It is in accord with this that he says: *A righteous and good God is unable to command the impossible; this indicates to us that we should do what is easy and ask help with what is difficult—for everything is easy for love* (Augustine, *De nat. et gratia,* chap. 69).[8] And elsewhere (*De perfect. just.,* chap. 10): *Who does not know that what is done by love is not difficult?*[9]

It would be useless to deploy more passages about this. Having shown you that the Council did not imply that the righteous are unobstructedly able to observe the commandments in the future, it will be easy for you to see that it was not able to claim that to be so—not only that it did not, but that it was not able to do so.

This is what appears clearly in canon twenty-two; it forbids, under pain of anathema, saying that all the righteous are able to persevere in righteousness; but does that not entail that not all the righteous are unobstructedly able to observe the commandments in the next moment, because there is no difference between the ability to keep the commandments in the next moment and the ability to persevere in righteousness—for persevering in righteousness is nothing other than observing the commandments in the next moment?

This definition in the twenty-second canon also entails that the righteous are not always unobstructedly able to persevere in prayer; for although the promises of the Gospel, and of Scripture, assure us of unfailingly obtaining the righteousness necessary for salvation if we ask

---

Chifflet, 34. The marginal citations common in seventeenth-century editions of conciliar texts have no magisterial authority.

    8. Augustine, *De natura* 69.83 (also in §§9, 10, 14, 15), from Sinnich, 177.

    9. Augustine, *De perfectione* 10.21 (also in §§10, 14), from Sinnich, 177.

for it in the spirit of grace, as we should, it is beyond doubt that there is no difference between persevering in prayer and persevering in the receipt of righteousness; and so it would follow that if all the righteous were unobstructedly able to persevere in prayer, they would also all be unobstructedly able to persevere in righteousness, which cannot be refused to their prayer. And that is formally contrary to what is determined by the canon.

And does not that same determination also contain as a necessary consequence that it is not true that God never leaves the righteous without the ability unobstructedly sufficient for prayer at the unobstructedly next moment, because there is no difference between being unobstructedly able to pray in the next instant and being unobstructedly able to persevere in prayer; and so, if all the righteous are unobstructedly able to pray in the next moment, then they are all unobstructedly able to persevere in prayer, and then they are all unobstructedly able to persevere in righteousness, against what the Council expressly says: the Council declares that the righteous lack not only perseverance, but even the ability to persevere without special help, which is to say help not shared by all?

From this you can see how much it is again necessary to conclude that it is true in one sense that God never leaves any of the righteous if they do not first leave God, which is to say that God never refuses grace to those who pray for it as they should and never distances himself from those who sincerely look for him; and yet, it is also true in another sense that God does sometimes leave the righteous before they leave him, which is to say that God does not always give the righteous unobstructed ability to persevere in prayer. For the Council declares that the righteous do not always have the ability to persevere, from which we have seen that it follows by necessity that it is opposed to the Council to say of any among the righteous that God gives them unobstructed ability to pray in the next moment; does it not then appear that there are some among the righteous whom God leaves without that ability, even while still righteous, which is to say before they have left God even by way of any venial sin?—because if God does not refuse this unobstructed help to any among them who have committed no venial sin since they were rectified, it would follow that all those who have been rectified would receive, along with their righteousness, unobstructed ability to persevere by way of general rather than special help.

From this we conclude that, following the Council, the commandments are always possible for the righteous in one sense, while in another they are sometimes impossible for them; and that God never leaves the righteous if they do not leave him, while in another sense God does sometimes first leave the righteous; you would need to be quite blind or not a little insincere to find a contradiction between these propositions, which hang so easily together—because to say that the commandments are always possible for love is nothing other than to say that not all the righteous always have the ability to persevere, which is in no way contradictory; and that God never refuses what is well asked of him in prayer, while God does not always give perseverance in prayer, which is not at all contradictory.

That is what I have to say to you on this subject, which I am very pleased to have undertaken to get you to see that verbally contradictory propositions are not always contradictory in sense. And because you have often thought to find a contradiction in the things I have had the privilege of speaking to you about, and because there are today people rash enough to suggest that there is a contradiction internal to the views of St. Augustine, I am unable to refuse such a convenient occasion fully to open to you the principles that so solidly bring into agreement all these apparently contradictory propositions, which are really bound together in wonderful sequence.

It is only necessary to remark that there are two ways in which we look for God, two ways in which God looks for us, two ways in which God leaves us, two in which we leave God, two in which we persevere, two in which God perseveres in doing good to us—and similarly for the rest.

The way God looks for us when he gives us faith's feeble beginnings so that in view of our lostness we cry to him, "*Lord, look for your servant,*"[10] which is to look for us so as to make himself found, is very different from how God looks for us when he answers that prayer. For those who say "*look for your servant*" have without doubt already been looked for and found. And it is because those who have the spirit of prophecy

10. Psalm 119:176.

well understand that there is another way in which God is able to look for them that they apply themselves to the first in order to get the second.

Similarly, the feeble way in which we look for God when he gives us the initial desire to leave our entanglements behind is very different from how we look for him when we move toward him, running in the path of his precepts after he has broken our bonds.[11]

All these things, which are not contested, lead us imperceptibly to consider things that are contested.

There are also two ways in which we persevere. Perseverance in prayer and entreaty simply for these strengths when we take ourselves to lack them is very different from perseverance in using these same forces and practicing these same virtues.

Similarly, there are two ways in which God leaves us, as we have already said—and similarly for the remainder.

Understanding these differences clarifies all difficulties and all apparent contradictions—which are not real because, of the two propositions that seem opposed, one has to do with one of the two ways, and the other with the other.

As we can consider righteousness in two ways, one with respect to its effects in particular cases, and the other with respect to its effects shared in common, so we can speak of it in two different ways. Who doubts that we can consider the initial light of faith separately from the actions that result from it? Or that we can consider faith and works in general and in some particular person, and accordingly speak of them differently? St. Augustine did this in order to accommodate himself to those he was speaking to when he said: *We can distinguish faith from works as we distinguish Judah from Israel in the kingdom of the Hebrews, even though Judah is Israel.*[12]

Is it not also in this way that St. Thomas, speaking of the gratuitous predestination about which you have no difficulty, says that we can consider it either in general or in its effects in particular cases, and can thereby speak in two contrary ways? When considering it in terms of its effects in particular cases we can specify causes, those that come first being the meritorious causes of the second, and those that follow being

11. Echoing, perhaps, Psalm 119:32.

12. Augustine, *De praedestinatione* 7.12, from Sinnich, 490.

the final cause of the former; but when considering all particular effects together, they have no other cause than the divine will; which is to say, as St. Thomas explains, that grace is given in order to merit glory, and glory because it has been merited by grace; but glory and grace together have no other cause than the divine will.[13]

Similarly, if we consider the Christian life, which is nothing other than holy desire according to St. Augustine, we find that God precedes us and that we precede God; that God gives without demand, and that God gives what he demands; that God works without our cooperation, and that we cooperate with God; that glory is both grace and recompense; that God leaves first, and that we do; that God is unable to save us without us, and that it has nothing to do with what we will or what we run toward, but only with God, who has mercy.[14]

By this you can see that almost everything the semi-Pelagians have said about righteousness in general is true of its effects in particular cases. This means that we can say the same as they do without being of their opinion, because the same propositions have different objects. In this way all the following expressions are shared by St. Augustine and his adversaries:

The commandments are always possible for the just;[15] *God does not save us without our cooperation;*[16] *we shall keep the commandments if we will to;*[17] *we are able to keep the commandments;*[18] *we are able to change*

13. The discussion in this paragraph responds to St. Thomas, *Summa Theologiae* 1.23.5, corpus. Pascal's immediate source for this mention of Thomas remains unclear. A similar point, though appealing to *Summa Theologiae* 2–2.162.4, is in Bourzeis, *Lettre*, 42. For some discussion, see Mesnard, *Oeuvres*, 3:561.

14. This paragraph contains summary statements foreshadowing themes to come. Several of them echo, distantly, quotations or allusions made more explicit and precise elsewhere in the *Writings*. Others, though they resonate with later quotations, often with more than one, are best read as Pascal's formulations. Two, however, are close to a particular source: (1) *nothing other than holy desire*: Augustine, *In epistulam Johannis* 4.6, from Sinnich, 430; (2) *what we will or what we run toward*: an echo of Romans 9:16.

15. Pascal's distillation of the eleventh chapter of Trent's Decree on Rectification, though see the discussion of *toujours* in §2.

16. Echoing Augustine, *Sermones* 156.12.13, from Sinnich, 172; and Prosper, *Epistula ad Demetriadem* 15 (also in §§10, 14), from Sinnich, 172.

17. Augustine, *De gratia et libero arbitrio* 15.31 (also in §9), from Sinnich, 180; Augustine quotes Ecclesiasticus 15:16.

18. Perhaps also an echo of Augustine, *De gratia et libero arbitrio* 15.31 (also in §9), from Sinnich, 180.

our wills for the better;[19] *glory is given to those who merit it;*[20] *ask and you shall receive;*[21] *I wait upon the Lord;*[22] *I precede the Lord;*[23] *not all are saved, because they do not will it;*[24] *God does not leave if he is not left;*[25] *God wills all to be saved;*[26] and so on.

All discourse of this kind is shared by both parties, St. Augustine as much as his enemies. How could it not be so, since most of this is scriptural?

But the contrary expressions are particular to St. Augustine and his disciples, such as: *salvation depends only upon God;*[27] *glory is gratuitous;*[28] *it is not those who will or those who run, but God alone who has mercy;*[29] *it is not by works but by call;*[30] *it is God who works—will and action follow his good pleasure;*[31] *the commandments are not always possible;*[32] *grace is not given to all;*[33] *not all are saved, not because we do not will it but because God does not;*[34] *each action we do in God is done in us by God himself.*[35]

Everything of this sort is proper to St. Augustine in such a way that, by a wonderful advantage of his doctrine, semi-Pelagian expressions are also Augustinian, but not the reverse.

19. Drawing from Augustine, *Retractationes* 1.22.4 (also in §§5, 9, 12), from Sinnich, 246–47; Augustine quotes his own *Contra Admimantum* 26 (also in §§5, 9, 12).

20. Echoing Augustine, *De correptione* 13.41, from Sinnich, 6/1.

21. Matthew 7:7; John 16:24.

22. Psalm 40:2.

23. Psalm 119:147.

24. Augustine, *Contra Julianum* 4.8.42, from Sinnich, 449–50.

25. Prosper, *Ad capitula* 14, from Bourzeis, *Lettre*, 15–16.

26. 1 Timothy 2:4.

27. Perhaps depending upon Augustine *De gratia et libero arbitrio* 8.20–9.21, from Sinnich, 668–69.

28. Probably an echo of Augustine's *De gratia et libero arbitrio* 8.20, from Sinnich, 668–69.

29. Romans 9:16.

30. Romans 9:12.

31. Philippians 2:13.

32. Pascal's distillation of the eleventh chapter of Trent's Decree on Rectification, though see the discussion of *toujours* in §2.

33. Augustine, *Epistulae* 217.5.16, from Sinnich, 725.

34. Augustine, *Epistulae* 217.6.19, from Sinnich, 727; Augustine resonates with 1 Timothy 2:4.

35. Fulgentius, *Ad Monimum* 9, from Sinnich, 489.

From this we can see how unjust it is to claim that those scriptural passages which seem to favor the semi-Pelagians bring the views of St. Augustine to ruin—for all these passages can have two senses; rather, those passages which establish St. Augustine's doctrine necessarily bring the semi-Pelagians to ruin because they are univocal, which is what St. Prosper says in writing a discourse to Rufinus on the same subject (chap. 3).[36]

36. Pascal read Prosper's *Epistula ad Rufinum* as it appeared in Latin and French in the second edition of Sacy, 282–85.

2^1

═══

The object of this discourse is to show the true sense of the words of the holy Fathers and of the Council of Trent:

The commandments are not impossible for the righteous.

One of these two senses is the true one:

(1) that it is not impossible for the righteous to accomplish the commandments;
(2) that the commandments are always possible for all the righteous by full and final ability to act, for which nothing is lacking from God.

The methods we will use to determine which of these two is the true sense are:

(1) first, to examine by way of the proposition's terms what sense we naturally take it to express;
(2) second, to examine by way of the purpose the Fathers and the Council had in arriving at this decision which of the two senses they had in mind;
(3) third, to examine which of the two is the true sense by way of the rest of their discourse, and by way of other passages from the Fathers and the Council which explain it.

1. I translate §2 from Le Guern, *Oeuvres*, 2:220–33; see also Mesnard, *Oeuvres*, 3:748–65. Miel, 210–11, translates a few brief excerpts from §2 into English. As in §1, unidentified italicized sentences and phrases are Pascal's quotations from, allusions to, or distillations of the Council of Trent's Decree on Rectification, together with its associated canons. He consulted the Latin text of the decrees and canons of that council in Chifflet, 24–49.

I hope that we see here that the terms of this proposition express and formulate only the first sense:

that the Fathers' and the Council's purpose was to establish only the first sense;

that the remainder of their discourse, together with an infinite number of other passages, explains these words in the same sense;

that the proofs they provide of this proposition conclude with no other sense;

that the conclusion they draw from their proofs implies this same sense by using other entirely univocal words;

that they have never formally established the second sense anywhere in their works;

and that not only have they formally established the first sense, but have also formally brought the second to ruin;

I doubt, after so many proofs, the possibility of doubting that they had in mind only the first sense.

We therefore divide this discourse into <...> sections.[2]

In the first—

First Method: To examine the proposition's
sense by way of simple terms. That the terms
of the proposition contain only the first sense.

No long discourse is necessary to show that the terms of the proposition *the commandments are not impossible for the righteous* contain only the sense *it is not impossible for the righteous to observe the commandments*; and that they do not at all imply *all the righteous always have full and complete ability to accomplish the precepts, for which nothing is lacking from God.*

Simple understanding of the language shows no rules of grammar by which to claim that to say something is not impossible is also to say *that it is always possible with full and final ability*. That is because its occasional possibility suffices to show that it is not impossible, without requiring that it always be possible.

---

2. Pascal appears to have left a space here for the number of sections into which §2 was to be divided, and never to have filled it in.

If there is need to clarify something so clear by way of examples, is it not true that it is not impossible for us to make war? And yet we are not all always able to do that.

It is not impossible that a prince of the blood should become king, and yet such princes are not always fully able to do that.

It is not impossible for us to live sixty years, and yet we are not all fully able to arrive at that age, or even to assure ourselves of a single instant of life.

Finally, to remain within the terms of our topic, the commandments are not impossible for us, and yet it would be a Pelagian error to say that all of us, even those weighed down by offenses, are always fully and finally able to accomplish the commandments.

It is enough that it is evident that the commandments are not impossible for the righteous; it is not necessary that all the righteous are always fully and finally able to accomplish them.

Those who so understand this determination of the Council think important the word *always* that their interpretation supposes. I hope that those who do not fear to use this passage with the word *always* recall the curse that threatens those who add to the words of the Holy Spirit;[3] and that those who quote more faithfully do not let themselves add to the sense, bearing in mind that God does not punish only those who do things, but also those who consent to them.

Second Method: To examine the sense
of the words by object, and so on.

Suppose it demonstrable that the Fathers and the Council, in refuting the error that *the commandments are impossible for us* in the sense that impossibility is absolute and invincible, had simply said in opposition that *the commandments are not impossible for us*; then it would be true beyond doubt that no one could claim that they had done anything other than deny what had been affirmed, and in exactly the same sense, which is to say that they would have established that *it is not impossible*

---

3. Pascal perhaps indicates here Proverbs 30:6, and Revelation 22:18.

for us to keep the precepts; and it would be ridiculous to say that such a determination implies a continuous and accomplished ability actually to keep the commandments.

It is evident, for example, that if some say it is impossible to live fifty years without being ill, those who simply affirm that, on the contrary, it is not impossible to live fifty years without being ill, have done nothing other than deny what had been affirmed, and in the same sense, which is to say that they have denied an absolute impossibility without however establishing by that denial a continuous and complete ability to live to that age without indisposition.

That being the general state of things, the only further issue about this particular topic is to show that the Fathers and the Councils had to combat the error, *the commandments are impossible for the righteous with an invincible impossibility*, in order to make everyone understand that the contrary proposition they established has no other sense than that *it is not impossible that the righteous observe the commandments*.

I will not pause to show that the Council of Trent had to refute heretics who made that mistake, because the heresy is known to be that of Luther. Those heretics are still with us, and so there can be no doubt. And so, it is no longer possible to contest that the sense of the Council's decision opposes that of Luther, and that it denies the impossibility of observing the precepts as that heresiarch meant it, which is to say, in the first sense.

But it is claimed that the same cannot be said about the identical determination found among the Fathers, because then there were no heretics with that opinion; because they spoke before that error came to be, what they said could not have been limited to that first sense by any circumstance; and so what they said should be taken generally and understood in the second sense: *the righteous are always entirely able to accomplish the commandments*.

That is the way some undertake to explain the meaning of the holy Fathers, and they make such a performance of their reasoning that it matters very much to bring it to ruin by overturning the sole basis of this interpretation.

What they say supposes three things:

first, that the Fathers did not have in mind heretics who held the invincible impossibility of the precepts;

second, that without heretics who held that error they could have had no other motive to oppose it;

third, that having no reason to bring it to ruin they would not have undertaken to do so because they would then have been combatting chimeras by refuting errors no one held.

It is necessary to reply by overturning these three fundamental assumptions with three particular responses.

First, if as yet no one had spoken of this error, the Fathers would not have left aside its condemnation if occasion for it had offered; this does not require saying that they would have been combatting chimeras.

Second, if as yet there were no heretics who held this error the Fathers could have had other reasons for opposing it: they might have heard it imputed to themselves, and been placed by that calumny under necessity of refuting the view as a matter of self-defense; that is in fact the case, and you would have to lack any understanding of the history of the Pelagian controversy and the writings of the holy Fathers to doubt the continual reproaches of the heretics who attributed that error to them.

Third, the Fathers had heretics in mind, namely the Manichees, who held that error as a principal dogma of their doctrine; that Luther did not invent it, but renewed it—that *the commandments are absolutely impossible*, that we have no free choice, that we must necessarily sin, that we are under an invincible incapacity to avoid sinning.

In this way, these three proofs taken together show that the Fathers were obliged to establish the proposition that *the commandments are not impossible* in the sense that it is not impossible that we observe them, not only for the considerations given by the Council, but for additional reasons: they had similar heretics to persuade, and more outrageous insults to repel.

Proofs of the First Point—Because the Church
often condemns errors held by no heretics without
this implying that she combats chimeras; and that the
Fathers could thus very well have established that
the precepts are not impossible in the sense that it is
not impossible that we observe them, even when
there had yet been no heresy of contrary opinion.

I do not know what empty reasoning leads to the claim that the Church is unable to remove evils by digging out the roots of heresies before their birth without exposing herself to the gibe that she combats chimeras.

Is it not enough that an error should truly be one for it to be a worthy object of her zeal?—why must she wait to condemn it until it has slipped into her children's hearts?

Shall we banish from her wise and prudent conduct the foresight so essential to and useful for prudence? And by what strange reversal does salutary vigilance, praiseworthy among individuals, in families, in states and every kind of government, all of which are transient, become ridiculous in the Church, whose care is far otherwise extended because of the assurance that she will last forever?

What I am combatting truly is a chimera; there is nothing more empty than its reasoning. The Church looks on the children promised her in every century as if they were present; gathering them all to her breast, she looks for rules of conduct for those yet to come as for those who have gone; by foresight as unlimited as the love she brings them, she prepares for them the means of their salvation with as much love as for those she presently nourishes.

Also, the Church is not concerned only to oppose present errors, nor, when occasion presents, to prevent those that have not yet appeared; but also to continue to condemn those already extinguished in order to prevent their eventual rebirth.

The councils provide examples of all these. We see that Trent condemns the opinion that *the righteous are able to persevere without grace,* even though the Lutherans, who were the only living enemies she was attacking, were far from having that purely Pelagian view. But today we feel the effects of that decision, apparently so little needed then and so very useful now.

Similarly, the Council of Orange condemns those who might dare to say that God predestines some to bad actions, even though it shows by its words that it is not aware that such an error has ever been made.

(*Conc. Araus.*, II, c. 25.)

Similarly, the Council of Valence confirms the same condemnation without supposing that the view is held by any, but only to prevent that evil from happening.

(*Conc. Valent.*, c. 3.)[4]

The holy Fathers, imitating such necessary prudence with similar zeal, have refuted in their writings errors not yet actual. How else can we oppose them when they do begin to appear?

Similarly, the holy Fathers who combatted Nestorius made public with holy joy the fact that St. Augustine had brought him to nothing before he was born, wondering at the particular providence of God for his Church to have in such holy fashion armed the writings of that holy doctor before the devil had armed that heresiarch with the errors St. Augustine combatted.

Saint Prosper.[5]

It would be useless to deploy more examples. It is sufficiently clear from what has been said here, that it is not possible to conclude from the fact that a heresy as yet has no followers that it is false that the Fathers could oppose it. From this we can draw the conclusion relevant to the topic under discussion here.

4. For these mentions of canons from the Second Council of Orange and the Third Council of Valence, Pascal probably depends upon Arnauld, *Seconde lettre*, 122–24.

5. Perhaps Pascal here indicates that Prosper is the source of the thought expressed in the immediately preceding paragraph. He may have had in mind Prosper's epitaph for the heresies of Nestorius and Pelagius in *Carmen de ingratis*, as given, in Latin and French, in Sacy, 177–84 (verse), 263–64 (prose); or, possibly, Prosper's *De gratia Dei* 21, as given in Bourzeis, *Propositiones*, 22–23 (though also in Sinnich, 21).

Proofs of the Second Point—That the holy Fathers
who established that the commandments
are not impossible were obliged to establish this
in the sense that it is not impossible that we
observe them, even though there was no heresy
of contrary opinion—for the sole reason that the
Pelagians criticized them constantly as holding
that view, denying free choice, and affirming
that the commandments are absolutely impossible,
and that we sin by inevitable necessity.

We should not call into question that, if it is true that Pelagians constantly imposed the denial of free choice upon Catholics as well as holding the absolute impossibility of the precepts in such a way as to affirm an inevitable necessity that forces us to sin, such criticisms alone might be sufficient reason to oblige the holy doctors to refute those errors even if no heretics had held them—so that they would have to say that it is not impossible for us to observe the precepts in order to shut the mouths of those who dared so unjustly to impose on them an opposed view.

And so, in order to show that the Fathers were obliged to defend against them, it will be enough to show that these heretics constantly taxed them with such criticisms. And that is very easy to do.

The writings of the holy Fathers who defend grace are full of passages that bear witness to this state of affairs. We see in all their pages in what outrageous terms these heretics claimed that Catholics deny free choice and affirm the invincible impossibility of the commandments.

The Manichees, writes Julian, *with whom we no longer have anything to do—I wish to say to all of them that we do not agree that free choice perished with the sin of the first human, nor that no one any longer has the power to live virtuously while all are forced to sin by the necessity with which the flesh binds us.*[6]

Is it not necessary that St. Augustine should defend himself against this criticism and reply that he holds it not impossible for us to live virtuously, and that we are not under an inevitable necessity to sin?

---

6. Augustine, *Contra duas epistulas* 1.2.4, from Sinnich, 132; Augustine quotes Julian.

Elsewhere Julian writes:

We are always busy defending ourselves against this doctrine. The reason why we resist these prevaricators is that we affirm free choice to belong naturally to us all; it could not die because of Adam's sin, as all Holy Scripture confirms.[7]

Is it not necessary that St. Augustine should declare that he does not deny free choice, against these objections and those of Pelagius, namely—

We hold that this power of free choice is in all of us generally, Christians, Jews, and pagans; free choice is in all of us equally, by nature (by these words Pelagius wants to distinguish himself from Catholics, upon whom he imposes its denial), *but only among Christians is free choice helped by grace* (and by these last words, Pelagius wants to appear not different from Catholics).[8]

And Julian:

All Catholics recognize it (free choice) *except for you* (speaking of St. Augustine), *who deny it.*[9]

And elsewhere:

Those who fear being called Pelagians fall into Manicheism, and from the fear of a heretical name, they become Manichean in reality. Thinking to avoid a false infamy, they fall into a real offense.[10]

And Pelagius, opposing two contrary heretics in order to show that he holds a middle position where the truth ordinarily flourishes (131): *We recognize free choice,* he says, *in such a way, however, that it always needs the help of grace. Those who say, with Mani, that we are unable to avoid sin, and those who are sure, with Jovinian, that we are unable to commit it, err equally. Both deny freedom; instead of this, we hold that we always have the ability both to sin and not to, so as sincerely to acknowledge that we are not deprived of free choice.*[11]

---

7. Augustine, *Contra duas epistulas* 1.15.29 (also in §14), from Sinnich, 132; Augustine quotes Julian.

8. Augustine, *De gratia Christi* 1.31.33 (also in §14), from Sinnich, 132; Augustine quotes Pelagius.

9. Augustine, *Contra Julianum opus imperfectum* 1.96 (also in §14), from Sinnich, 133; Augustine quotes Julian.

10. Augustine, *Contra Julianum opus imperfectum* 1.75 (also in §14), from Sinnich, 123; Augustine quotes Julian.

11. Pelagius, *Libellus fidei* 6, from Sinnich, 132; the parenthetical number in this paragraph is Pascal's reference to Sinnich, given erroneously.

And then St. Augustine, complaining about the error imposed on him:

Who is there among us who ever said that free choice died by the fall of the first among us? It is quite true that freedom dies because of sin, but that was the freedom reigning in the earthly paradise.[12]

And St. Prosper:

It is an error to say that free choice is nothing, or that it is not.[13]

And St. Augustine, to show that he does not deny freedom when he upholds grace:

It is, he says, *insupportably foolish on the part of our enemies to say that the grace we defend leaves no room for the will's freedom.*[14]

And elsewhere:

Free choice is not denied because it is helped; on the contrary, it is helped because it is not denied.[15]

And in the book *The Spirit and the Letter*, Chapter 29:

Do we bring free choice to ruin by grace? No; on the contrary we establish it in that way. For free choice is not brought to nothing but established by grace. As is also the case for the law and faith.[16]

And St. Prosper on the same subject in the *Letter to Demetrias*: *Should we fear that it seems that we deny free choice when we say that everything pleasing to God should be attributed to him?*[17]

And, reporting the Pelagians' words by which they mean to distinguish themselves from him:

The Pelagians, says St. Augustine, *take themselves to know something important when they say that God would not command things he knew we would be unable to observe. Who does not know that?*[18]

---

12. Augustine, *Contra duas epistulas* 1.2.5 (also in §14), from Sinnich, 137; Sinnich misattributes this excerpt to Prosper (as Le Guern also does, *Oeuvres*, 2:1223), an error which Pascal follows neither here nor in §14.

13. Prosper, *Responsiones* 6, from Sinnich, 139.

14. Prosper, *Epistula ad Rufinum* 8, from Sinnich, 137; Sinnich correctly attributes these words to Prosper; it is Pascal's mistake to attribute them to Augustine, a mistake he does not repeat when he provides the same excerpt in Latin in §14.

15. Augustine, *Epistulae* 157.2.10 (also in §14), from Sinnich, 140.

16. Augustine, *De spiritu* 30.52 (also in §14), from Sinnich, 141.

17. Prosper, *Epistula ad Demetriadem* 13, from Sinnich, 140.

18. Augustine, *De gratia et libero arbitrio* 16.32 (also in §§10, 12), from Sinnich, 180.

And elsewhere:

They think to oppose us with a very pressing claim when they say that we do not sin if we do not will to, and that God would not command something impossible for us to will. As if there were any among us ignorant of that![19]

And St. Jerome also needed to defend himself against the same arguments of the same heretics:

You object to us that God has commanded possibilities. Who denies it?

You like to say to us that either the commandments are possible, in which case it is just that they should be given; or impossible, and then breaking them should not be ascribed as a sin to those who have received the commandments, but to God, who gave them.[20]

And St. Augustine:

This is not at all the case—you are grossly deceived, or you are trying to catch out and deceive others. We do not at all deny free choice.[21]

It would be useless to report more proofs of a truth so clear—that those who defend grace were ceaselessly attacked with the complaint that they denied free choice; that they held the commandments to be absolutely impossible; and that we sin by invincible necessity—which is the Lutheran error. After which there is nothing clearer than the obligation they had to refute that error, just as much as the Fathers of the Council, because although as yet there were no heretics who held such errors, there were those who ascribed such errors to them with much assurance.

In order to confirm beyond possibility of defeat the need they had to act in this way, it is necessary to add that they really did have heretics for whom these were the principal errors, which completes the obligation to condemn such views. That is the topic of the third point.

19. Augustine, *De peccatorum meritis* 2.3.3 (also in §14), from Sinnich, 177.

20. Jerome, *Epistulae* 133.3 (also in §14), perhaps from Jerome, *Epistolae*, 266.

21. Augustine, *De nuptiis* 2.3.8 (also in §14), from Sinnich, 124.

Proof of the Third Point—That the Fathers
who established that the commandments are
not impossible were obliged to declare the sense
in which it is not impossible to keep them; that is
because they had to combat the Manichees,
who held to an absolute impossibility, and to an
inevitable necessity that forces us to sin

It is not possible to argue that the holy Fathers who established that the commandments are not impossible for us were not obliged to show in what sense it is not impossible that we observe them when there were present enemies who held the contrary—who denied free choice and held both that it is absolutely impossible for us to observe the commandments, and that there is an inevitable necessity that forces us to sin.

Further, who does not know that this is one of the Manichees' principal errors, and that the wicked nature they assert is such that there is no power capable of overcoming its evil, not even that of God?

Is it not known that St. Augustine refuted these errors, and that he won a very glorious victory over them for the Church? I will not pause to prove that here; it is necessary only to read what he wrote against these errors. I am content to report some passages in order not to leave the thing without proof, however well-known it might be.

Mani and others say that nature, which they call bad, can in no way be healed and made good.

It is miserably extravagant that he should take evil to be absolutely incapable of being changed.[22]

This is what makes Pelagius say:

We acknowledge free choice and the rest, and that they err who hold with Mani that we lack the ability not to sin.[23]

This is what makes Julian ceaselessly call St. Augustine and the Catholics Manichees, as appears in passages reported on the other point.

---

22. Pascal here combines two separate excerpts: Augustine, *Contra Julianum opus imperfectum* 1.97 (also in §14) and 1.115 (also in §14); both from Sinnich, 153.

23. Pelagius, *Libellus fidei* 6, from Sinnich, 132.

Julian:

With Mani, you deny free choice.[24]

And that is why St. Jerome, having said that the commandments are impossible without grace, guards against the ordinary heretical objection with these words:

You will at once accuse us of following Manichean dogma.[25]

It is therefore beyond doubt that everything Lutherans say about concupiscence was said about the evil nature by ancient heretics a thousand years before they existed. It is therefore not possible to argue that the Fathers were not forced to bring to ruin these horrible and impious views: that free choice is brought to nothing; that the precepts are invincibly impossible; that we are constrained necessarily and inevitably to sin; they were in fact obliged to do that, as much to overcome the error of those who held such views as to confound the calumny of those who ascribed such views to them.

It is no new thing that heretics have attributed to Catholics both the errors and the name of heretics opposed to them. *It is no surprising thing,* says St. Augustine, *that those who separate themselves from the Church give it new names; others have done the same when they have likewise separated themselves.*[26]

This is an ordinary artifice, shared by all the Church's enemies. Lutherans have used it in these recent times. They have imposed the name of Pelagians on the faithful, just as the Pelagians called them Manichees—which is to say, Lutherans. But the Church is not shaken by all these agitations. Changelessly holding to the power of grace against those who deny it, and to freedom against those who destroy it, she teaches to some that grace does not bring free choice to ruin, but on the contrary liberates it; and to others, that the cooperation of the will does not at all deny grace's efficacy, of which it is itself an effect.

And so it is clear that the Church opposes all the truths of which it is a repository to the falsehoods with which hell, unable to prevail against her, tries in vain to corrupt them; it is therefore possible neither

24. Augustine, *Contra Julianum opus imperfectum* 1.96 (also in §14), from Sinnich, 133; Augustine quotes Julian.

25. Jerome, *Epistulae* 133.4, perhaps from Jerome, *Epistolae*, 266.

26. Augustine, *Contra Julianum opus imperfectum* 1.6 (also in §14), from Sinnich, 125.

to claim that the Church ruins some points of the faith by others; nor that the Fathers have denied free choice in the categorical passages on grace's efficacy, as Luther claims; nor that they have ruined grace by those on free choice, because grace's efficacy and free choice subsist in perfect agreement; it is a lack of understanding of this that incites contrary errors. For, etc. etc.[27]

And so, this proposition which the Fathers have been forced to establish, *the commandments are not impossible,* is nothing other than the denial of the one imposed on them, *the commandments are absolutely impossible*; therefore, the Church excludes only the one sense, and says nothing else than that *it is not impossible for us to observe the precepts.*

Last Method

So many proofs make it sufficiently clear that the Manichees and the Lutherans make a similar error about the possibility of the precepts; and that they differ in that the Manichees attribute to a bad and incorrigible nature what the Lutherans ascribe to an invincible corruption of that nature; they nonetheless agree about the consequences: *we do not have free choice; we are constrained to sin by inevitable necessity; accordingly, the precepts are absolutely impossible for us.* In this way, differing only about causes and not about effects, which are the only things in question in this material, we can truly say that their views about the possibility of the precepts are similar, and that the Manichees were the Lutherans of their time as the Lutherans are the Manichees of ours.

Who, then, will be so blind as to not recognize that the Fathers then, and the Council of Trent in these recent times, had an equal and equally indispensable obligation to oppose to these impious views we have treated—that *the commandments are not impossible* in the sense given that claim by heretics?

Also, there is no sincere judge of this question who does not recognize such an evident truth; all those who have written about the

---

27. Le Guern, *Oeuvres*, 2:231–32, places this and the two paragraphs preceding it within brackets to indicate that they are struck through in the principal manuscript and indicated by a marginal note that reads *bon ailleurs*. See also Mesnard, *Oeuvres*, 3:762, for some discussion.

matter coolly have borne witness by their writing, from which it is easy to gather many passages. I content myself, however, with this from Estius,[28] who shows both that the ancient Fathers refuted the impossibility of the precepts only in the Manichean sense to defend themselves against Pelagian reproaches; and that the Council of Trent did the same only in the Lutheran sense, which is the whole meaning of the discussion here, and which has already been too much clarified; I bring the discussion to an end with these words:[29]

Porro eam sententiam qua dicitur, Impossibile aliquid a Deo homini praeceptum, Pelagiani Catholicis odiose impingebant, et Catholici studiose a se repellebant, quod ea ad haeresim Manichaeorum pertineret ponentium hominem propter naturam malam ex qua compositus esset, non posse peccatum vitare.[30] Hoc autem ita damnatum Catholicis, ut non tantum ex malo principio, cujusmodi re vera nullum est, verum etiam ex corruptione naturae facta per Adam, negent homini simpliciter impossibile esse ut legem Dei impleat, quod cum natura et legi impossibile est possibile facit, immo et praestat gratia Dei per Christum. Hujus dogmatis[31] definitionem, et claram interpretationem videre licet in synodo Tridentina, sess. 6, cap. 11, et can. 18.[32] (Estius, lib. 3, distinct. 27, pa. 6.)

This proposition, that God commands things impossible for us, was odiously ascribed to Catholics by Pelagians, and refuted by Catholics with as much ardor because it belonged to the doctrine of the Manichees, who held that we cannot escape sinning because of the evil nature of which we are made. The Fathers, too, condemned that proposition in such a way as

28. Guillaume Estius, or William Hessels van Est (1542–1613), taught theology at Louvain and Douai. His commentaries on Paul's letters and on Lombard's *Sentences* are often quoted approvingly by theologians Pascal treats as authoritative and reliable. See the treatment of Estius in Arnauld, *Saints Pères*, 359–60, which Pascal had certainly read.

29. There is no paragraph break here in the original manuscript. What follows has been set off as a block quote for ease of reading.

30. Le Guern, *Oeuvres*, 2:233, lowercases *catholicis* and *catholici* in this sentence. I correct for consistency, and in light of Desmares, 63. See also Mesnard, *Oeuvres*, 3:764.

31. Le Guern, *Oeuvres*, 2:233, reads *dogmati*. I correct in light of Desmares, 64. See also Mesnard, *Oeuvres*, 3:764.

32. This excerpt is from Estius's commentary on the *Sentences*; Pascal very probably draws it from Desmares, 63–64.

to deny the simple impossibility of observing the precepts, whether that is attributed to an evil principle, which is not real, or to a corruption of nature produced by Adam. Whether observing the precepts is impossible to nature or to law, the grace of Jesus Christ nevertheless makes it possible and accomplishes it. That doctrine is defined and explained clearly in the sixth session, the eleventh chapter, and the eighteenth canon, of the Council of Trent.

$$\S 3^1$$

===

The True Sense of the Words of the Holy Fathers
and of the Council of Trent: the commandments
are not impossible for the righteous.

Having shown so clearly that the true sense of the Council with respect to the possibility of the precepts is that they are possible with grace and impossible without it; and that grace's help, which renders the precepts possible with that full and final ability to act for which there is nothing lacking from God, is present or absent for the righteous as it pleases God, who, according to the opaque principles of his wisdom, need neither give it to nor take it from anyone—having shown all that, it doubtless seems strange to find treated here the particular question of the sense of a single, isolated passage, *the commandments are not impossible for the righteous,* which is in itself so obvious; the passage signifies simply that it is not impossible that the righteous should accomplish the precepts because it is not impossible that God give them that ability, as Lutherans claim it to be.

But what requires this clarification is the resistance to truth of those warned of the false doctrine that God always gives the help necessary to the righteous for the accomplishment of the precepts, help in which there is nothing lacking from him; they want to make this doctrine pass for that of the Council and the Fathers, based on nothing more than the claim that the commandments are not impossible for the righteous.

1. I translate §3 from Le Guern, *Oeuvres,* 2:234–35; see also Mesnard, *Oeuvres,* 3:746–47. Italicized sentences and phrases in §3 whose source is not noted are quotations from the eleventh chapter of Trent's Decree on Rectification, taken by Pascal from Chifflet, 33–34; or they are Pascal's distillations of the contents of that chapter.

In order to overturn that single basis for their view, it is necessary to declare the state of the question clearly, together with the methods proper to its resolution.

Second Section—The purpose of the
Council of Trent and the holy Fathers
in the decision that the commandments
are not impossible for the just

The purpose of the Council of Trent in this decision is beyond question. It is clear that the Church, then assembled against Luther, engaged his error about righteousness in its sixth session, and that in the eleventh chapter, its purpose was to combat these two errors: *the righteous are dispensed from observing the precepts*; and the other, its basis, *the commandments are impossible for the righteous.*

This being so, it would be useless to report proofs of it and ridiculous to ask for them. The thing is clear in itself, as the opening lines of the chapter show:

That none, however rectified they have become, should consider themselves exempt from the observance of the precepts; these words bring the claimed dispensation to ruin; and in order to bring to ruin the basis of that claimed dispensation, which is the claim that it is impossible to observe the commandments, the Council at once adds: *None should advance the proposition condemned by the holy Fathers, that the commandments are impossible*, etc.

The thing is in itself so evident that, etc.

§4[1]

Explanation of the Passage from the Eleventh Chapter of the Sixth Session: that the commandments are not impossible for the righteous.

The commandments are not impossible for the righteous—the sense of these words is sufficiently clear that it is strange to undertake an explicit clarification of them. It is evident enough that the words signify that it is not impossible that the righteous should observe the commandments, which is to say that it is not impossible that the righteous should do good works, which is what the same Council says in other terms in this very chapter.

But today there are people who refuse this entirely natural and truly proper sense in favor of the claim that the commandments are always possible for the righteous by an unobstructed ability for action, for which there is nothing lacking from God; by this interpretation, they add either the word *always* to the Council's decision, as most of them do, or the sense of that word, as all of them do; and so, it is to the point to get them to understand that this corrupts the sense of the proposition, not only against the rules of grammar, but also against the Council's intention and against the explanation the Council gives at the place where these words are found.

As to the first, that this interpretation is contrary to the rules of grammar, the thing is clear. That is because there is a considerable

---

1. I translate §4 from Le Guern, *Oeuvres*, 2:235–40; see also Mesnard, *Oeuvres*, 3:717–22. Italicized words in §4 whose source is not identified in these notes are Pascal's quotations or distillations of the eleventh chapter of Trent's Decree on Rectification, together with its canons. He relies upon Chifflet, 24–49, for the conciliar texts.

difference between saying that the commandments are not impossible and saying that they are always possible with complete and final ability; this is so clear that the following example shows that no proof is necessary: it is not impossible that someone might live one hundred years, but nevertheless no one has complete and final ability to do that.

They give to the words from the eleventh chapter, *the commandments are not impossible for the righteous*, the sense that the commandments are always possible for the righteous with complete and final ability, from which it follows that everything not impossible is always possible. Instead, the true and single sense of the words is that the commandments are not impossible for the righteous when they are helped by grace, as the Council explains everywhere—that is to say, in order to use words without equivocation, that the righteous, when aided by this help, are able to act well without sin.

What follows in the Council's discussion shows that this latter sense is the true one, as appears from the following proofs:

(1) From the purpose of the Council in this decision, which was simply to bring Luther's heresy to ruin, opposed as it is only to this latter sense.

(2) By the proofs the Council gives of the matter, which apply only to this latter sense.

(3) By the conclusion the Council draws, which expresses only this sense, in univocal terms.

(4) By the relevant canons, which express only this sense.

(5) By the same canons, which exclude and anathematize the former sense.

After that, it is surely not possible to doubt that this is the Council's sole sense.

Further, everything I say appears from a simple reading of this eleventh chapter, together with canons eighteen, twenty-two, and twenty-five.

For the intention of the Council, to oppose Luther's pernicious maxim, *the righteous are dispensed from the precepts*, appears in the first words of this chapter:

None, however rectified, should consider themselves exempt from observing the precepts.

And then, to bring to ruin the source of that error, which consists in the claimed invincible impossibility of accomplishing the precepts with grace, and of doing good works, the Council continues in these terms:

None should advance the proposition, anathematized by the Fathers, that keeping the commandments is impossible.

As it is only Lutherans who hold the absolute impossibility of the precepts, this decision is directed only against them, and not against the proposition *the commandments are impossible for the righteous who lack grace.*

It is just this that the Council establishes, striking with an anathema those who do not confess it. The Council, therefore, does not imply by this expression that the commandments are always possible with final and complete ability, for elsewhere it determines the contrary position, and there is no question of that in this place. The Council does not have in mind heretics who might say that the precepts are sometimes impossible, against whom they might have to oppose a contrary position—that the precepts are always possible—but only those who hold that the precepts are absolutely impossible, against whom the Council simply determines that love and actual grace are able to render the precepts possible. And that is what it expresses by saying that *the precepts are not impossible*, and proves by saying that:

For God does not command impossible things.

This reason well shows that the commandments are not absolutely impossible, but not that the righteous always have all the help necessary to accomplish them. To show that God is not unjust in imposing the commandments, it suffices that grace is able to render them possible; we need only have recourse to him to acquire the ability to observe them.

Also, there is no doubt that those laden with offenses lack grace. The precepts do not cease to obligate those in such a condition, even though they are not possible for them with the complete ability necessary.

And this is why the Council continues in this way:

God, in imposing them, warns you to do what you are able to do and to ask for what you are not able to do.

Therefore, God sometimes does command what we are as yet unable to do—

and he gives help so that we are able to—

Therefore, God gives to those who ask it the help they lacked when they received the commandments.

And his precepts are not burdensome, because God's children love Jesus Christ, and those who love him keep his commandments.

What do all the precepts indicate, except that those who have actual love can accomplish them? And so that we should not take the Council to mean habitual love, it at once adds to the words of Scripture[2] some that explain them:

which truly they are able to accomplish with God's help.

With these words, the Council joins to sanctifying grace, which makes us God's children, actual help, to provide ability to accomplish the commandments.

Who doubts, therefore, that the Council intends anything other than that the commandments are possible for the righteous, provided that God helps them? This is contested only by Lutherans, who are the only ones the Council had to combat.

Then the Council declares that the righteous are not always free from venial sins, but that such sins do not destroy their righteousness. It then reports several scriptural passages which show that it is not impossible for saints helped by grace to accomplish the precepts, and concludes like this:

from which it follows necessarily—whence it is certain—*that those who hold that the righteous sin in everything they do oppose the truth of the faith.*

It is easy to judge from this that since the Council has thought to conclude with the words, *therefore the righteous do not sin in everything they do*, what it had proposed with the words, *the commandments are not impossible for the righteous*, intends nothing other than that it is not impossible that the righteous sometimes observe the precepts, not that they are always able to observe them; otherwise, it would neither have proved nor brought to a close what it proposed.

It is the same thing to say that we do not always sin as to say that it is sometimes possible to accomplish the precepts. But to say that we do not always sin and that we are always able to accomplish the precepts is to say two very different things; there is no difficulty about that.

---

2. That is, John 14:23, embedded in Trent's text.

Finally, the three following canons, which summarize this doctrine with complete clarity, say not only that the commandments are only possible for the righteous with grace, but that they are only possible with special help.

Canon eighteen: *Any who say that keeping the commandments is impossible for all, even when rectified and established in grace, are to be anathematized.*

Canon twenty-two: *Any who say that the righteous are able to persevere without God's special help, or that they are unable to do so with that help, are to be anathematized.*

Canon twenty-five.[3]

From these canons, we see not only that the words *the commandments are possible for the righteous* are restricted to the condition of those helped by grace, but also that the affirmation of this possibility has only the same force as the claim that *the righteous do not sin in all their actions.* And lastly, that it is just as mistaken to extend unobstructed ability to all the righteous as it is forbidden to attribute special help to those who lack it; for such special help is not common to all, as has been explained.

Conclusion

Conclude, therefore, about these entirely holy decisions, that God mercifully gives complete and perfect ability to accomplish the precepts to the righteous when it pleases him, and, by just though hidden judgment, does not always give it.

Learn by means of such pure doctrine to defend together natural power against Lutherans, and natural powerlessness against Pelagians; the strength of grace against Lutherans, and the necessity of grace against Pelagians; not to bring free choice to ruin by grace, like Lutherans, and not to bring grace to ruin by free choice, like Pelagians. And do not think it sufficient to avoid only one of these errors in order to be in the truth.

---

3. Pascal does not provide the text of canon twenty-five here; Le Guern, *Oeuvres*, 2:239, gives it within brackets. Pascal does give the text of the canon in §1.

§5[1]

That possibility does not entail ability.

We are not always able to do everything possible for us. And although it is easy enough to avoid the thought that the one entails the other, there is nothing more facile and commonplace than to think that it does.

It is not that the connection is anything but ordinary; the mistake lies in taking it to be universal and necessary. Here are some examples of the connection, and of its absence:

A prince is legitimate heir to a kingdom, and is recognized as the true king by all his subjects, without division or opposition. It is at once possible for him to become king, and within his ability to do so.

Similarly, it is possible for the healthy and free to run when it pleases them, and they are also able to do so.

In these examples, possibility and ability are connected.

But it is also possible for us to live sixty years, and yet none of us has the ability to live to that age or to assure ourselves of a moment of life.

It is possible for a prince of the blood, even the last of a royal house, to become the legitimate king, without always being able to do so.

And so it is as easy as it is ordinary to see that the one may occur both with and without the other. From this it follows that the connection between them is neither constant nor necessary.

Therefore, by the force of words alone there is no necessary and persuasive opposition between saying that the commandments are possible for us and that we nevertheless are not always able to accomplish

---

1. I translate §5 from Le Guern, *Oeuvres*, 2:240–50; see also Mesnard, *Oeuvres*, 3:723–36.

them because the grace by which they are made possible for us is not always and necessarily with each of us.

In the same way, there is no difficulty at all in saying at the same time that healthy but chained people are able to run because their chains might be broken; and that they are unable always to run because their freedom does not depend solely upon themselves.

The same applies to sickness, and to a thousand other examples.

Rule for discerning the circumstances in which there is a relation between possibility and ability.

It is easy to decide by a general rule in what circumstances there is a relation between possibility and ability. In this way:

Whenever a cause that may produce an effect is present and under the control of those in whom it may be produced, there is a connection between possibility and ability. That is to say, when the subject is able to produce the effect, and not otherwise.

In this way, legitimate heirs to a kingdom received with acclaim by all their subjects are able to be monarchs, or not to; because everything is disposed to recognize them, it is their will alone that causes and controls what happens and since they alone dispose of their wills, they are said to have the power to produce the effect.

Things are not the same for captives held in irons; their freedom is certainly possible, but it is not within their power because the breaking of their chains, which is the cause capable of freeing them, does not depend on them. And so, we cannot say that they are able to leave their captivity, however possible that might be in itself.

That according to this rule we can always say that all are able to keep the precepts.

This rule, which seems to distance the accomplishment of the precepts from what any of us is able to do, on the contrary approaches exactly that, and places their keeping within our control.

This is so because the immediate cause of keeping the precepts is our will, so that, as already written, we keep them and break them at will; it is clear that this cause is always with us and depends upon us; following this rule, we ought not deny that each of us is always able to keep the precepts.

That according to this same rule, we are not always able to keep the precepts.

What is strange is that according to this same rule we are not always able to keep the precepts. For again, although the immediate cause of keeping the commandments is our will, there is nevertheless another cause in play, a first, dominant, and controlling cause exactly of our will—namely grace, God's actual help.

And because that first and principal cause resides not in us but in God, and depends not on us but on God, it is clear that in this sense we are not always able to keep the commandments.

Because of that pattern of reasoning, we do not contest that the infidels, abandoned to the excesses of their ungodliness and disorder, destitute of the help necessary for accomplishing the precepts, and subject to the full measure of their offenses, are in no condition to be able to keep the precepts.

And so, with respect to those very same ones of whom it is possible to say in an orthodox sense that they are able to keep the commandments—if they willed to, they could—it is said also in a Catholic and orthodox sense that they are unable to do so, because the lack of grace removes them from the will to do so.

That there are possible and impossible states of affairs which become otherwise according to circumstance.

It is therefore clear that the qualities *being possible* and *being impossible* belong together in many subjects according to the different senses given to the terms. It is also possible to imagine circumstances which might exclude one of these conditions.

Accordingly, we can say of healthy people in chains that it is not impossible for them to run, because the breaking of their chains, which would give them that possibility, has a cause in nature, but they are unable to run because that cause is not at their disposal; on the other hand, considering captives as captives, it can absolutely be said that so long as they are in chains, their escape is so impossible that it is not possible in any sense; that supposition completely excludes the cause of their freedom.

It is this that St. Thomas indicates with the word *incompossible* when he says that it is possible that someone might sin mortally, be elect, and be killed at each moment of life; but that it is nevertheless absolutely and always the case that those suppositions are incompossible at a particular time—that such a person might at once be elect, in mortal sin, and killed in that condition.[2]

Similarly, we can say of those with good eyes that they are able to see light when it is there if they will to do so; but not in any sense that they are unable to see light which is present if they absolutely will to do so.

In just the same way, we can say of the righteous who have all the graces necessary for the accomplishment of the precepts, and who have left everything else behind in order actually to accomplish them, that with no other help they accomplish them sometimes—that they are, according to that supposition, able to accomplish them, so that there is no other sense, all those circumstances being in place, according to which we can say that they are unable to accomplish them, or that it is impossible for them to do so.

In contrast, and in a similar way, we can say of the righteous, supposing them destitute of the help necessary to will to accomplish the commandments, that they are unable to accomplish them—and that in such a way that we cannot in any sense say, when imagining such a circumstance, that they are able to accomplish them.

2. In this paragraph Pascal seems to draw on two distinct passages from Thomas's *Summa Theologiae*: 1.23.6 ad 2, and 1–2.10.4 ad 3. It is likely that he took, or at least came to know of, the second passage from Bourzeis, *Propositiones*, 21, but it is unclear where he took the first passage from. It is also possible that Pascal consulted an edition of the *Summa* directly, but if so, it is not clear which. For discussion, see Miel, 85–86, and Mesnard, *Oeuvres*, 3:726–27.

For this reason, the Council of Trent, in order to present the truth directly and apart from contrary and repugnant errors, formulated two important decisions; by one, it established that the righteous are able to persevere when they have grace, and by the other that they are unable to persevere when they lack grace.—Canon eighteen—Canon twenty-two[3]—

These two decisions alone, the one constraining the consequences of the other, are able firmly to instruct the faithful: in making reference to ability or lack of it on the part of those who keep the commandments—not natural capacity or the lack of it, but the presence or absence of grace—the Council neither elevated nature too much, like Pelagians, nor degraded it too much, like Lutherans, but established the true reign of grace in our souls, as true Christians should.

These two decisions, too, only confirm what the Fathers had established for centuries past by way of these holy maxims:

Si Deus miseretur, etiam volumus;[4]

Si Deus tangit cor, homo praeparat cor;[5] (*De praedest sanctor.*, c. 8) *Si audisset et didicisset a Patre, veniret.*[6]

(*De grat. Chr.*, c. 14) *Quando Deus docet non per Legis litteram, sed per Spiritus gratiam, ita docet, ut quod quisque didicerit non tantum cognoscendo videat, sed etiam volendo appetat, agendoque perficiat.*[7]

(*Lib. 2, Oper. imperf.*, n. 157) *Cum vero dat incrementum Deus, sine dubio credit et proficit.*[8]

Tunc ergo efficimur vere liberi, cum Deus nos fingit, id est, format et

3. Pascal does not provide the text of these two canons here, but does in §§1, 4.

4. "If God has mercy, then we also will"—Augustine, *Ad Simplicianum* 1.2.12, from Sinnich, 389.

5. "If God touches our hearts, then we prepare them"—Augustine, *Contra duas epistulas* 2.9.19, from Sinnich, 424–25.

6. "If we have heard and been instructed by God, we will come"—Augustine, *De praedestinatione* 8.13, from Sinnich, 466.

7. "When God teaches not by the law's letter but by the Spirit's grace, he teaches so that whoever is taught does not only see by knowing, but also reaches out by willing, and perfects by acting"—Augustine, *De gratia Christi* 1.14.15, from Sinnich, 466.

8. "Certainly, when God gives increase, we believe without doubt, and progress"—Augustine, *Contra Julianum opus imperfectum* 2.157, from Sinnich, 466; Augustine echoes 1 Corinthians 3:7.

creat, non ut homines, quod jam fecit, sed ut boni homines simus, quod nunc sua gratia facit.[9]

All these expressions of the Fathers, to which the Council's decisions conform, clearly show that the righteous are able to accomplish the precepts with grace, and not without it—if they have grace, and not if they do not; when they have grace, and not when they do not.

There is room for hope here that such holy teaching might forever stifle the opposed errors of Luther and the Pelagians, together with all those that might come to be with something of their spirit.

It is nevertheless the case that those resolved to establish as an inviolable article of faith that all the righteous are always completely able to accomplish the commandments have not been restrained from doing so by sufficiently explicit condemnations. They elude them by ridiculous and ungodly artifice, which it is necessary to place in evidence in order to uncover all their evil and expose it to the judgment of the faithful. Here is their foundation –

The Council, they say, appropriately decides that the righteous are unable to persevere without grace, but it does not say, they claim, that such grace is ever lacking to the righteous. From the absence of such a statement, they undertake to establish the doctrine that such grace is always present to the righteous, and that by such help they are always able to accomplish the commandments.

It is not that the Council ever says that such grace is always present; it is only that it has not determined, as they would have liked it to do, whether such grace is always, never, or sometimes present; and so they have taken themselves to have the freedom to say, without injuring the Council's definition, that grace is never absent, and then to conclude, without combatting the definition, that the righteous are always completely able to accomplish the commandments.

If we ask them to prove this view and to indicate the Council's explicit passages that express it, they inevitably remain silent; but they also claim to be equally incapable of being refuted, and think they have

9. "Therefore, we become truly free when God fashions us, that is, forms and creates us, not as the human beings he has already made, but so that we might become good human beings, which he now effects by grace"—Augustine, *Enchiridion* 9.31, from Sinnich, 659.

done enough by cloaking themselves in an obscurity that removes from their adversaries the means of persuading them, while removing from themselves any means of proving their view.

And what is wonderful is that, not content to remain with probabilities by taking this opinion as tenable, they also want to make it pass as the Council's true view, and as a truth of faith; this is the topic of all today's disputes. When impunity favors their progress, arrogance and error intertwine easily and increase rapidly.

To bring all the useless subtlety[10] of their reasoning to a halt, it is enough to say to them that their view is not founded upon explicit determinations that support it, but rather upon the absence of those that condemn it; not upon formally expressed statements, but upon lack of contrary ones; not upon solid and palpable truth, but upon emptiness; not upon propositions, but upon supposition—and so those who oppose this supposition with a contrary one are able to do so with as much reason and support as they have.

To bring their useless subtlety to a halt, then, and to make them see the absurdity and ridiculousness of their way of corrupting the Council, it is necessary to propose something similar to them, so that they might clearly recognize in others the passions that impel them toward the opinion they have embraced, passions they do not see in their own case. The result will be that they will see a discourse similar to their own, offered today by those who undertake to introduce a new opinion and to accommodate it to the Council's terms.

"We submit ourselves to the Council and we anathematize the Lutherans and all those who say that it is not possible to accomplish the commandments when helped by grace; but, because the Council has only defended the necessity of grace to keep the commandments, without declaring whether it is ever present, we are left free to say that it never is present, and on this supposition to hold, without injuring the Council's definition, the unbroken impossibility of keeping the commandments."[11]

---

10. Le Guern, *Oeuvres*, 2:246 (and see Mesnard, *Oeuvres*, 3:730), marks *subtilité* here as a conjectural addition, presumably in light of the opening of the next paragraph.

11. This paragraph is Pascal's imagination of a position formally identical in its relation to what the Council of Trent explicitly says with the assertion that the

Truly, what should they say to us Catholics about such an extravagant opinion? That they find it entirely conformable to the Council? That they judge it entirely submissive to the Council? And how would they put up with someone who wanted both to make it pass as the Council's true sense, as the one true faith, and as supportable and probable?

Should one not rather protest, with reason, that this would be to play with the Holy Spirit's words; that there is no considerable difference between this error and Luther's because the two agree about the impossibility of the commandments even if they differ as to the cause of that impossibility; that it is anathematized, and should be choked as a pernicious and detestable monster?

I entreat those with such zeal for religion not to cool it off, but to leave it unchecked, and, without confining it to this topic alone, to extend it to all who similarly injure the Church. That is because I suppose their ardor to have its source in love for the truth and not in hatred for a particular error, with the result that everything equally false is to them equally odious.

They should consider now what they are doing with their opinion, and whether it is not a perfect imitation of what they detest in others. They must be blind if they do not see the perfect conformity, or very unjust if they do not partake of their aversion—for they should have similar opinions about entirely similar topics.

Recognize sincerely, therefore, that the very holy truths God has placed in his Church ought not be in the least corrupted in this way, and that it is an entirely unworthy and outrageous abuse to claim that the Council, in undertaking to destroy heresies about the absolute possibility and absolute impossibility of keeping the precepts, has established power to keep the precepts against the one, and lack of power to keep them against the other—which would be to arrive nowhere.

That would not have been very fitting, useful, etc.

If the word *possible* has such an extended meaning, that of *ability* is no less extended. Is it not evident that if it is said that something is

---

commandments are always possible. It serves as a reductio of the attempt to reconcile the particular understanding of the commandments' possibility with the text of Trent, which Pascal is arguing against.

within our power if it is done when we will to do it and not done when we do not, then nothing is so much within our power as our own will?

It is in this sense that it is true that all are able to accomplish the commandments: it is certain that in order to keep them, they need do nothing other than will to do so: *Si vis, conservabis mandata.*[12]

St. Augustine has also said that all of us are able, if we will, to turn ourselves away from the love of temporal things toward the keeping of God's commandments, without thereby permitting the Pelagians to claim that this accords with their maxims. *Because,* says this Father, *while it is true that each of us can do this if we will to, the will is prepared by the Lord.*[13]

Elsewhere, he again says that it is within our power to alter and correct our wills without this doing an injury to the grace he has preached; that is because he has made clear that this power is nothing if not given by God; *Because,* he says, *just as something is said to be within our power if we do it when we will to, nothing is more within our power than our own will; but the will is prepared by the Lord, and it is in that way that he gives the power. This is how it is necessary to understand,* continues this holy doctor, *what I said elsewhere: "it is within our power to deserve to receive the effects of God's mercy or anger,"* because the only thing within our power is what comes from our will: when God prepares it thoroughly and powerfully, godly action otherwise difficult or impossible becomes easy.[14]

It is therefore very clear that when the word *ability* is taken in this way, all of us have it to accomplish the precepts. However, it is also true, in another sense, that those without instruction, like the infidels, lack ability to accomplish the commandments because they are ignorant of them. How can they acquit themselves of an obligation they do not know to have been imposed upon them? How can they invoke what they do not believe in? How can they believe in what they have not

---

12. "If you want to, you will keep the precepts"—echoing Matthew 19:17.

13. In this paragraph, Pascal partly summarizes and partly quotes from Augustine, *Retractationes* 1.10.2, from Sinnich, 246; Augustine echoes Proverbs 8:35.

14. Augustine, *Retractationes* 1.22.4 (also in §§1, 9, 12), from Sinnich, 246–47; Augustine quotes his own *Contra Adimantum* 26 (also in §§1, 5, 12), and echoes Proverbs 8:35.

heard spoken of? How can they hear it spoken without a preacher?[15]

And this accords with what St. Augustine says: *It is necessary and inevitable that those ignorant of righteousness violate it—Necesse est ut peccet a quo ignoretur justitia.*[16] And elsewhere: *You can rightly say to someone, 'You can persevere, if you will to, in things you have grasped and held.' But you cannot at all say, 'You can believe, if you will to, in things you have not heard spoken of '.*[17] From this it is evident that Christians instructed in God's law are, because of that knowledge, because they know their master's will, able to accomplish the commandments in a way not shared with those who lack such instruction. It depends only on their consent to obey it.

One can say of the righteous with yet more reason that they are always able to keep the commandments because their will is free from the bonds that held it captive; they also find the will cured of languor, (though there remains some weakness in it, which means that, with the Fathers, we cannot say that their wills are free, healthy, and strong);[18] it is evident that they are able to keep the commandments in a way that is not shared with those who, being in servitude to the love of creatures, are opposed to God and subject to passions that prevent them from following and observing the law.

For in the same way that one says of an eye that it is able to see when it has no interior indisposition that prevents it from doing so, it is also possible truly to say of the will of those disengaged from the passions that previously dominated them, that it is then able to love God.

It is not that the will does not still have need of grace's help, however healthy it is, because, as St. Augustine says, *In the same way that the eye, even though perfectly healthy, cannot see if not helped by light, so we, however perfectly rectified, cannot live in piety if not divinely assisted by the eternal light of righteousness.*[19]

---

15. This paragraph contains echoes of Romans 10:16.

16. Augustine, *Contra Julianum opus imperfectum* 1.108, from Sinnich, 181.

17. Augustine, *De correptione* 7.11, from Sinnich, 679.

18. Pascal here denies that it is proper to say of the wills of the baptized (*les justes*) that they are *libre, saine et forte*, even though they have been *dégagée des liens qui la retenaient captive, et se trouvant guérie de ses langueurs.* It is possible, by contrast, to say of (the wills of) Eve and Adam that they are *juste, sain, fort.* See the discussion in §11.

19. Augustine, *De natura* 26.29, from Sinnich, 336 (though see next note).

Nevertheless, as one does not cease to say that the healthy eye is able to see when considering that faculty in itself, because it has no need of more health in order to see, but only external light, so also it is possible to say of the rectified soul that it is able to love God when considering the soul in itself, *because,* as St. Thomas says, *it has no need of more rectification in order to love God, but only of active helps.*[20]

It is however necessary that these active helps should be such that (Augustine, l.1 *Oper. imperf.*) *delight in love exceeds delight in sin, otherwise the result would be that delight in evil would continue without being vanquished, always tempting those it holds in slavery; for we are in servitude to what vanquishes us and we will certainly always be vanquished if not helped by God so that we not only understand what we need, but also so that the soul, being healed, vanquishes and overcomes in us delight in things desire to possess which or fear of losing which makes us sin.*[21]

Nevertheless, one can say of those who are helped by grace, *even if less than necessary for them to continue perfectly in God's way,*[22] that they have an ability they would not have were they deprived of all help, because to have a part of what is needed is much closer to having it all than having nothing would be. And even when this imperfect help is too weak for a temptation one faces, it may become strong enough if the temptation diminishes, and then the temptation will be effectively vanquished, which would not happen were one without help. Similarly, one can say of those whose vision has been weakened by illness, and who need a lot of light, that though a little light does not make them

20. It is probable, though not certain, that Pascal draws both the immediately preceding quotation from Augustine (*De natura* 26.29) and the discussion of Thomas from *Summa Theologiae* 1–2.109.9, where the quotation from Augustine is in the sed contra and the view that Pascal attributes to Thomas in the corpus. It is not clear, however, in which seventeenth-century edition of the *Summa* he read this text, if indeed it was from such an edition that he took these quotations.

21. Pascal here combines two excerpts: (1) Augustine, *Contra Julianum opus imperfectum* 1.109 (also in §13), from Sinnich, 119; (2) Augustine, *Enchiridion* 22.81 (also in §13), from Sinnich, 102.

22. Le Guern, *Oeuvres*, 2:250, and Mesnard, *Oeuvres*, 3:735, both italicize this phrase, following in this, they say, the principal manuscript, in which the words are underlined. It seems likely, then, that someone (Pascal? A copyist?) once thought this phrase a quotation or near-quotation; but the editors indicate that they have not traced its source, as I also have not.

completely able to see, it nonetheless gives a certain kind or degree of ability they would not have had were they in darkness—very close to everything necessary in such a case; and, too, if their health strengthens, that light might become strong enough to give them complete ability to see.

There are, then, these many ways of thinking about different abilities; they are all accurate, even though the only way of being able to do something that can be called entire, complete, and perfect, and which provides the action itself, is the one lacking nothing for the act. And so it is entirely true that one can say of those who lack any help, without which it is certain they will never act, that they are unable, in this sense, to act.

In the same way, it is true to say that those in darkness are unable to see—that is, when considering complete and final ability, without which they will not act.

And so, however righteous people might be, if they are not helped by powerful enough grace, or, to use the Council's words, *by God's special help,*[23] then it is true, according to the same Council, that they are unable to persevere because, although they are able to persevere in the diverse senses already explained, they nevertheless lack complete and final ability to act, for which nothing is lacking from God. That is why the Council forbids, on pain of anathema, saying that they have such ability.

23. Council of Trent, Decree on Rectification, canon twenty-two, from Chifflet, 46.

§6[1]

(Augustine 571) If, following St. Augustine, *God, by permission, or by providence and disposition, mixes the elect with those among the righteous who will not persevere so as to frighten those who remain with the fall of those who fail,*[2] there would be nothing so contrary to that plan of God as to give to those who are not failing a sufficiently unobstructed ability, and to assure them that they will always have it, with the result that the example of those who fail by using that ability badly would necessarily be utterly unable to frighten them. For if God did not remove that ability from any among the righteous, what consequence could follow from the fall of those who used it badly that could bring terror to the others, so that they would then be able to use it well? And is it not necessary that such a removal be entirely free on God's part, to make it so that when such ability is taken away from some among the righteous, those who are not more righteous than they might have reason to fear a similar result from their master? But if they themselves are assured of keeping this help as long as they keep their righteousness, and if they are assured of not losing this help except by using it badly, how is it possible for them to be brought to humility by the example of others—for there would be none among those others who could make them fear in any way other than by using their ability badly, which it is not in them to do?

(527) *Who knows in this life if they are predestined? It is necessary that this should be hidden in a world where pride is so much to be feared*

---

1. I translate §6 from Le Guern, *Oeuvres*, 2:251–56; see also Mesnard, *Oeuvres*, 3:708–16; Miel, 209–10, translates a few excerpts from §6 into English. All parenthetical numbers in §6 are Pascal's references to pages of Sinnich.

2. Augustine, *Epistulae* 217.4.14, from Sinnich, 571.

that a very great apostle was struck by an angel of Satan out of fear that he might aggrandize himself. It is for this reason that Jesus Christ said to those very apostles, "If you remain in me"—even though the one who said this was sure that they would remain; and the prophet: "If you will, and if you hear me"—even though he was sure that they would both act and will to do so. And many similar things are said because of the usefulness of this secret.[3]

If, therefore, it is necessary to think that it is in service to the usefulness of this secret that righteousness is given to some among the reprobate, who are not removed from this Christian life until they fall, so that the elect might learn that they never have assurance of perseverance; and that fear is necessary not only before righteousness, but also after it—does it not follow that the righteous lack unobstructed ability to endure?

If therefore it is a firm principle for St. Augustine that the righteous lack assurance of perseverance, how can they be given assurance of the presence of unobstructed ability to pray, the right use of which assures them of receiving what they ask for? Is it not clear that it is to go against the opinion not only of St. Augustine but of the whole Church without exception, and even of those very people who importune you to the contrary, that no one ever has assurance of persevering, that the most righteous are not free from this fear, and that nothing would so bring righteousness to ruin as the ruin of this fear? For how could that fear remain with the righteous if they were sure they were always unobstructedly able to pray, sure also that the Gospel assures them they will always get what they ask for with righteousness?

Can there be anything more contrary to common sense, and to truth? It would not only be fear that would be destroyed for them, but also hope, for as we do not hope for something certain, we also will not hope for the continuation of this help because it is certain for us; also, hope, for us, will not be to get what we ask for, because that too is certain. What then will be the object of our hope other than ourselves, for whom we hope good use of an ability of which we are assured?

---

3. Augustine, *De correptione* 13.40, from Sinnich, 527; Augustine quotes or echoes, in order, 2 Corinthians 12:7 (Paul is the *grand Apôtre*), John 15:7, and Isaiah 1:19.

112[4]

Because the sole reason for which God sometimes gives delight to the righteous and sometimes does not is so that all understand it as a gift of God and have their vanity cured, what is more opposed to this than saying that such delight is always present?

113[5]

And if it is to make them humble that even the saints are only tardily healed of some vices, what is more contrary to such humbling than to say that we are always able to ask for such healing?

You see that according to these new dogmas the righteous need neither fear nor hope, except in themselves. Also, the heretics who assert such dogmas interpret the passage *work out your salvation with fear*[6] to mean fear, not of God leaving you, but of not using graces well. Understand that these are their terms. Consequently, this fear is about what they are able to do by means of their will to use their ability well; for St. Paul, by contrast, it is about God himself working this will in us, not following the disposition of our will, but rather that of God's own good will.

Understand, then, following St. Augustine, that prayer is always the result of effective grace; that those who have this grace pray; that those who lack it do not pray, and do not have unobstructed ability to pray;

4. The page of Sinnich signaled by this number contains an excerpt from Augustine's *De peccatorum meritis* 2.17.27 (also in §§9, 13). The gravamen of the excerpt, which Pascal does not here supply, is that we sometimes do and delight in the good, and sometimes not, without knowing why. And that this state of affairs ought encourage us to see such doing and such delighting as gifts from God, which is to say not under our control. What Pascal writes immediately next seems to assume the content of the excerpt.

5. The page of Sininich signalled by this number contains an excerpt from Augustine's *De peccatorum meritis* 2.19.33 (also in §§9, 13), whose gravamen is that God's provision of grace for the healing of our vices occurs on a schedule opaque to us, and that this state of affairs ought encourage us to see such healing as merciful rather than required or entailed by our righteousness. What Pascal writes immediately next seems to assume the content of the excerpt.

6. Philippians 2:12.

that the extent to which God does not leave us without grace to pray is the extent to which we pray; that those who do not pray have been left without the ability to do so; that it is an incomprehensible mystery why God retains one and not the other of two righteous people; that those who persevere have effective help; that those who do not persevere lack unobstructed ability to do so; that free choice is no longer strong enough for perseverance; that God does not will to commit unobstructed ability to us; that perseverance among the angels is by way of unobstructed ability; that such ability is no longer with humans; that what was the result of our merits is now the effect of grace; that it no longer belongs to free choice to persevere; that such perseverance is the work of grace; that it is such work that effects prayer; that only prayer brings us to God; that only prayer does not distance us from God; that God wills it to be nothing other than prayer that does not distance us from him; that of all who persevere, none does so except by effective grace; that of all who do not persevere, there are none who, in their first detour from God, are not first left by God; that there is a great difference between the fall of the angels and the fall of the righteous now; that there is nothing incomprehensible about Adam's fall, but that the fall of the reprobate righteous is incomprehensible; that free choice no longer has strength to use unobstructed ability; and that free choice would be able to persevere only with such an ability. If righteousness is given to the reprobate only to keep the elect in fear; if the elect themselves are sometimes left by God in order to teach them fear and humility; and finally, if it is inconceivable why of two infants, twins if you like, but better said any, one is baptized and not the other, then it is yet more opaque why one of two righteous people perseveres and not the other—then acknowledge frankly that it is thoroughly false to follow the maxim that all the righteous are unobstructedly and sufficiently able to pray, because if that were so, the contrary of all I have been reporting about St. Augustine would necessarily follow, namely, that it would not be opaque why one of two righteous people perseveres while the other does not, and all the rest—which you can follow as easily by thinking as by reading.

Acknowledge frankly, therefore, the grandeur of this mystery: why one perseveres and another does not. In order to look at it in all its depth, you should clearly conceive that if God had willed to damn everyone, he would have exercised his righteousness; no mystery there. If he had effectively willed to save everyone, he would have exercised his mercy; no mystery there. And in willing to save some and not others, he has exercised both his mercy and his righteousness; no mystery there, either. But, when all are equally guilty, he has willed to save these and not those; there, properly, is the grandeur of the mystery. Consequently, if it is a great mystery that of two equally guilty, he saves this one and not that one without any reference to what they do, then certainly St. Augustine is right to say that the mystery of why God gives perseverance to one among the righteous and not to another is yet more surprising.

For it does not seem as strange that God refuses grace to a guilty one as that he refuses to retain a righteous one in grace. For in the one case, there are faults that attract exclusion from grace, while in the other there are none.

But this surprise ceases when we consider that God does not need to make us righteous with the same grace he used to make Adam righteous, and that so long as God gives Adam sufficient help in his initial condition, nothing requires God to give him everything he needed in the corruption into which he precipitated himself. For I have no doubt at all that God does not always give to all the righteous forces yet more powerful than those given to Adam; those forces can be as powerful as you like, so long as you acknowledge that they are sometimes insufficient to provide unobstructed ability.

If such help is now of as little use to us as the absence of any help at all, that is because the sin we have committed in Adam has made it in that way powerless. Consequently, because God is now no longer obliged to give these helps, we have nothing to complain about if we do not get them.

It is true that God obliges himself to give these helps to any who ask for them, and that is why those who ask are never refused. We ought not twist the meaning of this by saying that we get perseverance in prayer by asking for it, and that, therefore, we get grace to pray in the immediately next moment by asking for it now, in the present, and in that way, we are assured of persevering—that is playing with words.

God gives to those who ask, not to those who have asked, and that is why, in order to get it, it is necessary to persevere in asking. It does not suffice to ask today, with a pure spirit, for continence tomorrow; for if one subsequently becomes impure, who does not see that such a change of heart destroys the effect of the preceding prayer, and that to have continence tomorrow we must not cease asking for it? So, if in the present moment, we ask for the gift of prayer in the next moment, is it not clear that we will not get it if we do not continue to ask for it? Is not to say that we will have the spirit of prayer in the following moment, if we pray for it in that following moment, to say that we will have it if we will have it—and thus to play with words?

It is therefore established that God is obliged to give graces only to those who ask for them, and not to those who do not. And because we cannot ask for the grace of prayer without having it, it is apparent that God is not obliged to give grace to anyone, because no one can persevere in asking for it without continuing to have it.

But because God engages himself by his promises to give to the children of the promise even if they do not ask him, he engages himself to give exactly to them the grace to pray to get the grace to live well; but since obligation always follows promise, God has it only to those he has made promises to—which is to say, the predestined.

It is for this reason that, as all are ignorant whether they will be of that number, all should fear, because none among the righteous is incapable of falling at any time, just as any sinner may be lifted up at any time. The grace of prayer can at any time be given and taken away.

Those are the kinds of fear and hope that should continuously animate the saints. And that is why, following St. Augustine, Jesus Christ willed, being on the cross, to give a remarkable example of both the one and the other: the abandonment of St. Peter without grace, and the conversion of the thief by a prodigious effect of grace.

In accord with this, each of us should always humiliate ourselves under God's hand as poor, saying, with David, *Lord, I am poor and a beggar.*[7] Clearly, because he was a king, he did not speak of the good of riches. Neither, because he was a prophet and righteous, did he speak of the good of grace. In what, then, consisted the poverty of a man with

---

7. Psalm 40:18.

such abundance, other than that he could lose his abundance at any moment, and that he was unable to keep it? If he had had unobstructed ability to remain in that righteousness, what would have been lacking for him to call himself rich rather than poor?

There are certainly none able to be called poor if they have unobstructed ability to ask, together with assurance of receiving what they ask for. That is why all those who are poor unfailingly lack either ability to ask, or ability to receive. The poor in grace, however, are never unable to get what they ask for; they must, therefore, be unable to ask.

So, there is this difference between the poor in the order of nature and the poor in the order of grace: the poor of the world are always unobstructedly able to ask, but are never assured of receiving, while the poor in grace are always assured of receiving what they ask for, but never of being able to ask.

That is all I can say to you now with the little leisure and capacity I have. I pray God to make it useful to you for understanding his truth.

§7[1]

It is clearly established that many are damned and many saved. Also, that the saved willed to be, as did God; if God had not willed it, they would not have been saved, and if they had not themselves willed it, they would not have been saved. The one who made us without us cannot save us without us.[2] It is also true that the damned very much willed to perform the sins that merited their damnation, and that God, too, very much willed to condemn them.

It is evident, therefore, that God's will and ours concur in the salvation and damnation of the saved and the damned. There is no question about all these things.

If, therefore, we ask why some are saved and some damned, we can say that, in one sense, it is because God wills it, and in another because they do.

But it remains a question which of the two wills, God's or theirs, is superior, dominant, source, principle, and cause of the other.

It is a question, that is, whether our will causes God's, or God's ours. The one that dominates or is superior to the other may alone be so considered in a way: not because it is, but because it enframes the concurrence of the subordinate will. The action is then allotted to that initial will, and not to the other. It is not that the action cannot, in a sense, also be allotted to the subordinate will; but action belongs properly to the superior will, which is its principle. The subordinate will is such that we can, in one sense, say that action proceeds from it because it concurs in

1. I translate §7 from Le Guern, *Oeuvres*, 2:257–64; see also Mesnard, *Oeuvres*, 3:781–91; Levi & Levi, 213–20, provides a complete English rendering of §7; Miel, 202–3, translates a few excerpts from it, as does Krailsheimer, 27–29.

2. Perhaps echoing Augustine, *Sermones* 169.11.13 (also in §12), from Sinnich, 429.

that action; and in another sense, that action does not proceed from it, because it is not the action's source. But the primitive will is the one of which we can properly say that action comes from it, and cannot at all say that action does not come from it.

In accord with this, St. Paul says, *I live, not me but Jesus Christ lives in me.*[3] Certainly, the first words, *I live*, are not false, because he was alive and not only with corporeal life (which is not addressed here), but with spiritual life because he was in grace; he himself also says elsewhere in several places, *we were dead and have been brought to life.*[4] Although it is entirely true that he was alive, he at once denies it by saying, *I am not alive—non ego vivo.* The Apostle is not a liar. It is therefore true that he is alive, since he says, *I am alive.* It is therefore also true that he is not alive, as he says, *Jam non ego—I am not <alive>.* These two truths exist together because his life, even though properly his, does not come originally from him. He is alive only by Jesus Christ. Jesus Christ's life is the source of his and so, in a sense, he is alive because he has life; also in a sense he is not alive, because he has only another's life. It is true that Jesus Christ is alive, and we cannot say that he is not.

(*Jesus Christ does not will to be first; you will to be that.*)[5]

Accordingly, Jesus Christ himself says, *I do not do the works, but the Father who is in me,*[6] and yet also says elsewhere, *the works I have done.*[7] Jesus Christ is no liar, and his humility does not distort his truth. Because he says this, we can say that he did things and that he did not do them. But it is clearly established that the divinity in him did them, and we cannot say that it did not.

Accordingly, the prophet says, *O Lord, you have done all our works in us.*[8] Therefore, these works are God's because he did them, and ours because they belong to us.

3. Galatians 2:20.

4. Ephesians 2:5.

5. The parentheses indicate that this sentence is written in the manuscripts' margins. See Le Guern, *Oeuvres*, 2:258, and Mesnard, *Oeuvres*, 3:783. Although Le Guern italicizes the sentence, it seems best not to think of it as a quotation or allusion. Mesnard provides it only in a footnote.

6. John 14:10.

7. John 14:12.

8. Isaiah 26:12.

Accordingly, St. Paul says, *I have worked, not me but the grace of Jesus Christ that is with me.*[9] How has he worked and not worked, unless it is the grace with him that worked? The work, however, can also be said to be his because his will concurred with it; and it can be said to be not his because his will was not the source of the desires proper to himself. We can say that the grace of God worked because it prepared his will, because it effected volition and action in him; and we cannot say that it did not work, because it was the origin and source of his work.

Accordingly, St. Paul says elsewhere, *Non ego, sed quod inhabitat in me peccatum,*[10] speaking of the undeliberated movements of his will.

There are many examples in the Scriptures of this kind of talk; they show us that when two wills concur in a result, if one is the dominant, superior, and unfailing cause of the other, the action can be both attributed to and denied of the subordinate will and can be attributed without possibility of denial to the dominant.

We therefore consider the dominant will as alone, even though it is not, because it is alone in that we can attribute all action to it and cannot refuse to do so. Following this way of putting things, it is a question:

—whether what belongs to the saved and the damned comes from God's wanting it or their wanting it.

That is to say:

it is a question whether God, subjecting our wills to his, had an absolute will to save some and damn others; and whether, in consequence of this decree, he turned the wills of the elect toward good and those of the reprobate toward evil in order to conform them respectively to his absolute will to save and to damn.

Or whether, subjecting the use of his graces to our free choice, he foresaw how each would want to use it, and following their wills has shaped them for salvation or condemnation.

This is the question at the moment lively among us; it is decided differently by three schools.

The first are Calvinists, the second Molinists, and the third the followers of St. Augustine.

9. 1 Corinthians 15:10.

10. "Not I, but sin that lives in me"—Romans 7:20.

Calvinists[11]

The opinion of the Calvinists is:

- God, in creating us, created some to damn them and others to save them, by an absolute will and without foreseeing any merit.
- In order to execute that absolute will, God made Adam sin, not merely by permitting but by causing his fall.
- In God there is no difference between *doing* and *permitting.*
- God, having made Adam sin and all of us sin in him, sent Jesus Christ for the redemption of those he willed to save when creating them, and he gives them love and certain salvation.
- God abandons those he willed to damn when creating them, and deprives them of love through the entire course of their lives.

That is the appalling view of these heretics; it is injurious to God and insupportable by us. Those are the blasphemies by which they establish in God an absolute will to save or damn his creatures without any foresight of merit or sin.

Molinists

In hatred of this abominable opinion and of the excesses it contains, the Molinists took up a view not only opposed, which would have sufficed, but absolutely contrary. It is that God has a conditional and general will to save all of us. For this outcome, Jesus Christ was enfleshed to save all without exception; his graces are given to all, and whether they are used well or badly depends upon the will of the recipients, not upon God's. God, having foreseen from all eternity the good or bad use we would make of his graces solely by our free choice and without the help of a discriminating grace, willed to save those who would use the graces well and to damn those who would not, lacking on his part an absolute will to save or damn any.

This opinion, contrary to that of Calvinists, produces an entirely

11. Pascal's principal source for this discussion of the Calvinists is Bourzeis, *Saint Augustin victorieux,* 108–44.

contrary outcome. It flatters the common sense that Calvinists wound. It does that by making it master of salvation and fall. It excludes any absolute will from God, and makes salvation and damnation proceed from our will, instead of, as in Calvin's view, both salvation and damnation proceeding from the divine will.

These are the contrary errors between which the followers of St. Augustine, treading more restrainedly and with more thought, have established their view in the following way.

Followers of St. Augustine

These consider two states of human nature.

The first is the one created in Adam, healthy, unspotted, just, and right, coming from God's hands from which nothing can come except what is pure, holy, and perfect;

the other is the state to which it was reduced by the sin and rebellion of the first of us, which has made it in God's eyes soiled, abominable, and detestable.

In the state of innocence, God could not with righteousness damn any, and also could not refuse any the graces sufficient for their salvation.

In the state of corruption, God could with righteousness damn the whole entire mass, and even today those born without being removed from that mass of the damned by baptism are damned and deprived eternally of the beatific vision, which is the greatest of evils.

Following these two very different states, the followers of St. Augustine develop two different views about God's will for our salvation.

They claim that in the state of innocence, God had a general and conditional will to save all, provided that they would have willed it by free choice aided by the sufficient graces he gave them for their salvation, which did not, however, unfailingly determine them to persevere in the good.

But that Adam, having used that grace badly by free choice, and having rebelled against God by a movement of his will with no push from God (horrible to think), corrupted and infected the entire mass of humans so that it became the object of God's righteous anger and indignation. They add that God divided that mass, identically guilty and in its entirety worthy of damnation, so that he willed to save one part by an absolute will based upon his entirely pure and gratuitous mercy, and left the other part in the damnation where it was, and where he could, with righteousness, have left all of it, he foresaw both the particular sins that each would commit, or at least the original sin of which all are guilty, and consequent upon that foresight he willed to condemn them.

To bring this about, God sent Jesus Christ to save absolutely and by entirely effective means those whom he chose and predestined from that mass; these are none other than those he willed absolutely to merit salvation through Christ's death; he did not have the same will for the salvation of others; they have not been delivered from that universal and just perdition.

Nevertheless, for the benefit of the elect, some among those not predestined are not left aside from being called and, in that way, they participate in Jesus Christ's redemption. It is the fault of such people that they do not persevere; they could have if they had willed to do so, but, not being among the elect, God does not give them the effective graces without which they are in effect never able to will it. Consequently, there are three kinds of people: those who never come to faith; those who do, but, not persevering, die in mortal sin; and the last category, those who come to faith and persevere in it in love until death.[12] Jesus Christ had no absolute will that the first group should receive any grace by his death, with the result that they received none.

He did will to redeem the second group and gave them the graces that would have brought them to salvation had they used them well, but he did not will to give them the singular grace of perseverance, without which the graces given are never used well.

But as for the third group, Jesus Christ absolutely willed their salvation and brought them to it by certain and unfailing means.

Everyone is obliged to believe, though with a belief mixed with fear and unaccompanied by certitude, that they are among the small number of the elect whom Jesus Christ wills to save; and never to judge any

12. An echo of Matthew 13:1–23.

who live on the earth, however wicked and ungodly, so long as there remains to them a moment of life, that they are not among the number of the predestined, leaving the separation of the elect from the reprobate as God's impenetrable secret. This obliges everyone to do for all others what might contribute to their salvation.

That is their view. According to it, we see that God has an absolute will to save the saved, and a conditional will coupled with foresight to damn the damned; and that salvation comes from God's will, and damnation from ours.

That is the view of the followers of St. Augustine, or rather that of the Fathers, and of the entire tradition, and consequently the Church; the other views are to be considered wanderings of the human mind. Further, although it is a very sensible agony for the Church to see herself torn by opposing errors which combat her most holy truths—and although she must pity Molinists and Calvinists—she nevertheless recognizes that she is injured less by those who wander in their errors while remaining in her womb than by those who separate themselves to set one against another without any longer having affection for the maternal voice with which she calls them, or deference to the judgments with which she condemns them. The error of the Molinists afflicts her, while their submission consoles her; but the error of the Calvinists, coupled with their rebellion, makes her cry to God, *I nourished children and they have scorned me*.[13] She knows that, for Molinists, it is enough for her to speak through the mouths of her popes and councils, that the tradition of the church is venerated by them, that they do not undertake to give the words of Scripture idiosyncratic interpretations, and that they intend to follow the interpretations given them by the great crowd of the succession of holy doctors and popes and councils.

But the rebellion of Calvinists renders her inconsolable. She must act toward them as one equal to another; setting aside her authority, she must use reason. She nonetheless calls them all to herself, and prepares herself to win over each according to their proper principles.

She consoles herself by the fact that these contrary errors establish her truth—that to leave them to themselves is enough to destroy them,

---

13. Echoing Baruch 4:11–12.

and that the weapons her various enemies use against her cannot hurt her and can only bring their users to ruin.

It is not only in this encounter that she suffers opposed enemies. She has almost never been without this double combat, and as she has undergone this opposition with respect to the person of Jesus Christ, her head, whom some make merely human and others only God, she has experienced similar opposed enemies with respect to almost all the other tenets of her belief. But, imitating her head, she extends her arms to both the one and the other, calling them all; and she embraces them together to bring about a happy union.

She therefore addresses you and asks the topic of your complaints, and first to you, Molinists, as being among her children and …[14]

14. §7 trails off at this point.

§8[1]

In this way, it is said that God does not leave the righteous if they do not leave him. And yet he[2] shows in a number of places that God leaves first. The sincerity of good faith is needed to arrive at the true sense of these passages; the alternative is to be repelled by them and to blind oneself.

These two states of affairs subsist together: that sometimes God leaves first, and that sometimes we leave first. It is true that God does not cease to give help to those who do not cease to ask it; but it is also true that we would never cease to ask it if God had not ceased to give us grace to ask it of him, so that in considering this double cessation on God's part, one in which he ceases to give prayer, and the other in which he ceases to give the result of prayer—and it is also certain that God never ceases to give the result of prayer to those who ask for it— it is certain that we never cease to ask for it if God does not cease giving the asking for it to us.

This double desertion, one in which God precedes and the other in which God follows, is indicated clearly for us by St. Prosper when he says: *God does not leave if we do not leave him; and he often acts so that we do not leave him.* From this we must say that God does not always so act. So, among those for whom God does not act so that they do not leave, it is evident that God ceases in the first way, in not acting so that we do not leave, following which we leave God; and then God leaves us in the second way. If we then ask St. Prosper why it is that God retains

1. I translate §8 from Le Guern, *Oeuvres*, 2:264–75; see also Mesnard, *Oeuvres*, 3:693–707; Miel, 208–9, translates a few excerpts from §8 into English. All parenthetical numbers in §8 are Pascal's references to pages of Sinnich.

2. Presumably Augustine, as the context strongly suggests.

some and not others, he replies with the immediately following words: *Why does God retain these and not those? It is neither permissible to look for nor possible to find the answer to that.* From which we see that those God does not retain leave him, following which he leaves them—which is exactly what I said.[3]

St. Augustine, St. Prosper's master, teaches the same thing when, speaking generally of the fall of all those among the reprobate who arrived for a time at righteousness, he declares, *they receive grace, but temporarily, which is to say for a time. They leave and are left, for they have been abandoned to their free choice by a righteous but hidden judgment.* From this we see that the righteous leave God for a time before he leaves them, but the reason why they leave God is that *they have been abandoned by him to their free choice,* which is the same as what St. Prosper says and what I propose. You see here the two desertions, one in which God follows, which is not mysterious, and the other in which God precedes, which is entirely mysterious. I cannot stress this enough. But in order to make you see, when we lack formal passages, that it is so far beyond doubt in St. Augustine's doctrine that we would never leave God had God not left us, I want to get you to see that the contrary position can only endure by bringing all of St. Augustine's principles to ruin.[4]

Examine, therefore, if you will, this question at its root, because I know it to be the point that touches you most—see whether it is possible in the doctrine of these saints that the righteous can leave God before God has to some extent left them to themselves.

In order to do this, it is necessary to acknowledge as fundamental that God never leaves those who pray to him; on the contrary, he always accords them the means necessary to their salvation if they sincerely ask for them.

It is therefore not in question whether God ceases to give help to those who persevere in asking it, because this has never been thought.

But it is in question whether God ever ceases to give to the righteous

---

3. The italicized words in this paragraph are quotations from Prosper's *Ad capitula* 14, from Bourzeis, *Lettre,* 5–16.

4. The italicized words in this paragraph are quotations from Augustine, *De correptione* 13.42 (also in §§9, 12), from Bourzeis, *Lettre,* 29.

all the help necessary in order to pray. Let us now examine this according to St. Augustine's principles.

If we find it to be a firm principle for St. Augustine that all who actually pray do so by way of effective grace, and that none among those who do not actually pray are unobstructedly able to do so, the question is surely resolved; does it not follow necessarily that for as long as the righteous pray, they are effectively helped, and that they do not cease praying so long as this effective help remains with them, and that when they do cease, they lack unobstructed ability to pray? Consequently, God has left them first, I do not say with no help, but without unobstructed help. Certainly, this follows. See, then, whether I can prove these principles.

If we find it to be a firm principle in St. Augustine that not only important actions are God's gifts—no one today doubts this—but that prayer and faith, too, which are lesser things by which we adhere to God and without which we are sure to leave him, are also gifts, effects, and works of grace, occurring only by the express action of grace, this surely suffices to show that we only pray by a grace that brings prayer about. Perhaps you will deny this;—that although all the righteous have grace sufficient for prayer, it nonetheless happens that no one prays except by way of effective grace. And so, although prayer does not happen for anyone unless produced by grace, ability to pray is nonetheless found in all the righteous. But that is not tenable. It is a question of fact whether any among the righteous diminish their unobstructed ability to pray by what they do; that question can only be answered by information about all the righteous, specifically about how prayer takes shape among them. This means that it would be rash beyond relevance to be certain that prayer never fails to occur among the righteous, past and future, because of a diminution in their unobstructed ability produced by what they do. We cannot say the same about the Thomists' sufficient grace; that is to say that we can, without irrelevance, say that it is never diminished by what we do because the Thomists do not establish it as unobstructedly sufficient.[5] But if this claimed ability of the

5. Pascal probably has in mind Thomas, *Summa Theologiae* 1–2.109.9, corpus (also in §§5, 9); it is not clear where he read the text. For some discussion, see Mesnard, *Oeuvres*, 3:563–64, 734.

righteous to pray is unobstructed, it is not possible to say with confidence that not all those who pray do so by way of this unobstructed ability, but instead do so by way of effective grace. The upshot is that if St. Augustine and all the Fathers affirm that prayer is always a result of effective grace, it necessarily follows from such a universal claim that those who do not pray are not unobstructedly able to do so.

Therefore, to show that all who do not pray lack unobstructed ability to do so, it suffices to show that all who pray do so by effective grace. And that is what we find in all of St. Augustine, and in general elsewhere. It is why all his works on grace were written, almost without exception.

(Fulgentius, 160): *Grace, in order to be chosen, first chooses, and is neither received nor loved without itself working in our hearts. So, both reception of and desire for grace are works of grace.* And then: *Grace itself brings about understanding, love, desire, and asking.*[6]

(Fulgentius, 268): *We cannot have even the desire to pray unless it is given to us by God.*[7]

(Augustine, 438): *Those who take prayer to be ours rather than a gift to us should guard against self-deceit.* And then: *They do not want to understand that even our prayer is God's gift.*[8]

(Augustine, 438): *It is that selfsame one who makes us ask for what we want to get, look for what we want to find, and knock at the door we want to open.*[9]

(Augustine, 438): *Prayer itself is a gift of grace.*[10]

(Fulgentius, 490): *God gives us a good will so that we might want to believe in him, faith so that we might believe in him, and love so that we might love him.* And then: *It is grace alone which brings about good will in us; grace alone gives faith to that will.*[11]

It would be useless to report more witnesses; this is the entirety of the purpose of St. Augustine and his followers. Consider the strength of

6. Fulgentius, *De veritate praedestinationis* 1.15.33–1.16.34, from Sinnich, 160.

7. Fulgentius, *Epistulae* 6.6, from Sinnich, 278; Pascal gives the page number from Sinnich wrongly.

8. Augustine, *De dono* 23.64 (also in §9), from Sinnich, 438.

9. Augustine, *Enarrationes* 118.14.2 (also in §9), from Sinnich, 438.

10. Augustine, *Epistulae* 194.4.16 (also in §9), from Sinnich, 438.

11. Fulgentius, *De veritate praedestinationis* 1.18.38, from Sinnich, 490.

his expressions. If it is true that such grace is neither loved nor received except when it itself works that result in the heart, how is it possible to say that those who do not love God have unobstructed ability to do so, and that it depends upon them to love him, without effective grace?—rather, grace is loved only by way of its own efficacy. Would it not be absurdly extreme to say that prayer is a gift of grace, and that God makes us ask for all we want, if it is possible that we ask by way of unobstructed ability without grace making it so that we ask? How can one say that grace alone gives faith to the will if there are some with unobstructed ability for faith, from which it would follow that they had it and then diminished it by their actions, and so it would not, for them, be the case that grace alone gave it to them? You might perhaps say that it is almost impossible that the saints …[12]

To show by way of these explicit passages that the ability to pray is absent among those who do not pray, attend to St. Fulgentius (278): *It is not possible to have even the desire to pray if it is not given by God.*[13] Therefore, those without this desire also lack the ability to have it.

(Fulgentius, 178): *Therefore, when God commanded us to will, our need was indicated; but because we are not capable of this ourselves, we are advised to ask for that ability from the one who gives us the command about it, which, however, we are unable to ask for if God does not work that very will in us.*[14] Therefore, those who lack the will lack also the ability.

It is not that they lack a more distant ability, such as the possibility of being saved that we all have. For whenever we say that we lack the ability to do something, we do not always exclude more distant abilities—but we clearly do always exclude unobstructedly sufficient ability. Therefore, when it is said that we are unable to have the will to pray if it is not given by God, it is certain that the inability in question extends at least to unobstructed ability.

These passages, which formally exclude ability to those who do not act, are as strong as we can hope for. But that does not prevent those passages which do not formally exclude ability, and which do no more

12. This paragraph is clearly incomplete. See Le Guern, *Oeuvres*, 2:268.

13. Fulgentius, *Epistulae* 6.6, from Sinnich, 278.

14. Fulgentius, *De veritate praedestinationis* 2.4.6 (also in §§9, 10), from Sinnich, 178.

than attribute every act to the effectiveness of grace, from having unfailingly the same strength to exclude unobstructedly sufficient ability; and so it is no longer possible, as I have already said, to make the effectiveness of grace the sole cause of faith and prayer if all the righteous have unobstructedly sufficient ability to bring those things about.

Conclude, therefore, that all those who have faith and pray do so by effective grace; and that all those who lack these things lack the unobstructed ability to have them. It follows that all who persevere in prayer have effective grace, which makes it so that they both pray and persevere in prayer; and that all those who have that grace pray; while those who do not persevere in prayer are destitute of that effective grace, and of grace unobstructedly sufficient; and that those destitute of that sufficient grace do not pray; so that none among the righteous cease to pray unless their doing so follows upon God's making them destitute of the effective grace unobstructedly sufficient for prayer.

This major point of St. Augustine's doctrine is proved beyond refutation, both by the principle which here clarifies it, and by all the others.

If we find it to be a firm principle that the elect persevere to the end by entirely effective means, which is to say that the only ones who persevere to the end are those who do so by such means, does it not follow that none who do not persevere have unobstructed ability, by the reasoning just given? For if the reprobate who are righteous have unobstructed ability to persevere in prayer, and consequently to obtain perseverance in righteousness, how can one be sure that none who have persevered and are effectively persevering now do so only by entirely effective means, so that there is nothing absurd or impossible in the view that all who have unobstructed ability to persevere do so, and that, on the contrary, it is morally impossible that among the thousands who have that unobstructed ability there would not be at least one who diminishes it by what they do—when it is likely there would be many, and absolutely false that there could be certitude in saying that there would be none? If, therefore, St. Augustine has established positively that all the elect are saved by effective graces, and that all the righteous who are not elect will beyond doubt not persevere, is it not also beyond doubt that they lack unobstructed ability for such perseverance, for if they had it, it would be impertinent to affirm that it would never be diminished by what they do, because the essential property of unobstructed ability is to give us absolute certitude[15] about its diminishment by what we do. However, who does not know that it is a principle of this Father, widespread in all his works and fundamental to his doctrine, that the elect, which is to say all those who persevere, certainly do so by entirely effective means; and that the reprobate righteous certainly do not persevere.

If it is a firm principle in the doctrine of St. Augustine that Adam and the angels had unobstructed help sufficient for them not to distance themselves from God,—by means of which they were able either not to distance themselves, or, by distancing themselves, not to use that help—and that now these possibilities are not within the strength of our free choice because God wills them to belong only to grace so that only in that way can we approach him and not be distant from him— must we not then conclude from the difference between God's will with respect to innocent nature and corrupt nature, and from the difference in the means by which he gives it to us not to distance ourselves from him, that those who persevere do so by grace's effectiveness, and that those who do not persevere lack unobstructed ability to do so? And what is more familiar in St. Augustine's doctrine than the difference between these kinds of help?

Must we not conclude that God no longer wills, now, to hand over perseverance to our free choice, and that we are, now, no longer capable of using unobstructedly sufficient help? This is what St. Augustine establishes in all his books, particularly throughout *Correction and Grace*, and throughout most of *The Gift of Perseverance*.[16] From the latter, this summary suffices: *So that we do not distance ourselves from*

15. Le Guern, *Oeuvres*, 2:269, provides *certitude* here. Miel, 65, and Mesnard, *Oeuvres*, 3:700, argue that the correct reading must be *incertitude*. I follow Le Guern, however—the sense is that if you have unobstructed ability (and know that you do), you are thereby certain that (only) what you yourself do can diminish or remove said ability.

16. This is one of the places in the *Writings* that strongly suggests Pascal has acquaintance with Augustine's *De correptione* and *De dono* as a whole rather than solely by way of excerpts present in florilegia such as Sinnich, even though all excerpts from these works in the *Writings* are clearly drawn from there.

God he shows that such an action can only be given by God; it is in no way at the command of free choice. It was at such command for us before the Fall, and that freedom of the will belonged also to the excellence of that initial condition among the angels, who, when the Devil had fallen along with his own, remained close to the truth and merited to arrive at eternal assurance. But after our fall God willed that it would only be by his grace that we would approach him, and that it would only be by his grace that we would not remove ourselves from him.[17] From this we sufficiently see that the first human received unobstructedly sufficient help, (this is beyond doubt St. Augustine's doctrine, and if one doubts that, it is only necessary to have recourse to the book *Correction and Grace,* which is entirely concerned with this), by means of which he could either persevere or not, so that it was left to his free choice to use this power according to his will; St. Augustine then declares two things to us: that free choice in its present condition no longer has that ability; and that God no longer wills to commit perseverance to free choice, but wills that only by his grace is it possible to approach him, and that it is also only by his grace that we do not distance ourselves from him. Consider now whether there is anything more opposed to this doctrine than to say that God now gives the righteous unobstructed help to persevere, and that he has given it over to their free choice to not distance themselves from him. St. Augustine holds that free choice is not now capable of that unobstructed ability; while they[18] claim that free choice effectively has that unobstructed ability. St. Augustine says that God no longer wills that we do not distance ourselves from him by means of such an ability under the control of free choice, while the Molinists say that free choice does effectively have that unobstructed ability. St. Augustine says that God no longer wills to submit the ability not to distance ourselves from him to our free choice; the Molinists say that God does give just such an ability to us. St. Augustine says that unlike the holy angels, who merited glory by persevering through means of their free choice helped by such an ability, God wills now that apart

17. Augustine, *De dono* 7.13 (also in §9, twice), from Sinnich, 183.

18. The Molinists, as the context makes almost certain. See Le Guern, *Oeuvres,* 2:1230, and Mesnard, *Oeuvres,* 3:702. Subsequent occurrences of 'the Molinists' in this paragraph render Pascal's unspecified *ils.*

from grace, it no longer belongs to us not to distance ourselves from him; while the Molinists say that God gives the righteous just such an ability not to distance themselves from him.

You can see that St. Augustine's doctrine is very far from that; I think it impossible to fabricate a doctrine more formally contrary to it.

God does not will there to be anything other than his grace which might now make it so that we do not distance ourselves from him, which is to say so that we do not cease praying to him; by contrast, he left this to Adam's free choice. Can it be said that there are today any who persevere in prayer by means of that unobstructed help, when God has willed that it should not be so?

If free choice is now no longer capable of using unobstructed ability, and has no longer the strength to use it as Adam did, how could it be that it does use it?

And finally, to connect these two things: if God wills it not to be by such help that we do not distance ourselves from him, and that free choice be incapable of using such help, into what abyss of absurdity fall those who say that we avoid distancing ourselves from God by just such help?

Nothing better excludes unobstructed ability than ….[19]

If it is a firm principle of St. Augustine's doctrine that free choice is no longer capable of using unobstructedly sufficient help, must we not conclude that there is nothing more absurd than to say that the righteous have unobstructedly sufficient help to avoid distancing themselves from God in their prayer? Only those scarcely versed in these capital maxims do not know this.

The reason for our current incapacity to enter into equilibrium, that unobstructed balance between opposites which Adam had, is that Adam's free choice was not attracted by any concupiscence. His will, says St. Augustine, had nothing in it that was obstructed by concupiscence, which no one contests.[20] And so, being entirely free and not entangled, he was able either to remain in righteousness by way of unobstructedly sufficient help, or to distance himself without being forced or attracted by anything else. But now, in the corruption that

19. This paragraph is clearly incomplete. See Le Guern, *Oeuvres*, 2:271.
20. Perhaps responsive to Augustine, *De correptione* 12.34, from Sinnich, 667.

has infected soul and body, proliferating concupiscence has made us slaves of delight in it, so that, being enslaved to sin, we can be freed from that slavery only by a more powerful delight which enslaves us to righteousness.

Also, St. Paul's admirable teaching[21] should suffice to instruct us about this. He says that we are either slaves to righteousness and free from sin, or free from righteousness and slaves to sin; that is, we are enslaved either to righteousness or to sin; we are never without enslavement to one or the other; we are therefore never free from both.

We are now slaves to delight; what delights us more attracts us unfailingly. That is a principle so clear both to common sense and to St. Augustine that it cannot be denied without renouncing both of them.

For what is clearer than the proposition that we always do what delights us most? That is nothing other than to say that we always do what pleases us most, which is to say that we always want what pleases us, which is to say that we always want what we want, and that in the state to which our souls are now reduced it is inconceivable that they should want anything other than what it pleases them to want, which is to say what delights them most. We should not think to be subtle by saying that the will, in order to show its power, sometimes chooses what pleases it less, for in that case, it pleases it more to show its power than to will the good it leaves, so that when it forces itself to shun what pleases it, it is only to pursue what pleases it, it being impossible that it should want anything other than what pleases it to want.

This caused the following maxim to be established by St. Augustine as fundamental to the way the will works: *Quod amplius delectat, secundum id operemur necesse est*[22]—it is necessary that we work in accord with what delights us most. It is from this that the entirety of this discourse[23] flows.

That is how we are today slaves to delight. We unfailingly follow enslavement to flesh or spirit, and are freed from one only by the dominion of the other.

21. Probably in Romans 6:16–18.

22. Augustine, *Expositio* 49; Pascal's immediate source is unclear, but perhaps Jansenius, *Augustinus*, 3.4.6, col. 412.

23. Pascal may have Jansenius's *Augustinus* in mind as referent of *tous ces discours*; or perhaps his own writing.

It could be said that in placing the delights of the spirit on a par with the delights of the flesh, our souls recover their initial balance, or equilibrium, and that in such a condition they will again be free to choose between opposites that delight them equally, as Adam was free to determine his direction in the absence of delight.

But the response to that apparently significant objection is very easy. It is very true that free choice in that condition is driven neither by the one nor the other of the concupiscences, but it does not follow that it is free to go to the one or the other; only that it is unable to choose either the one or the other. For how can there be a choice between two equal delights for those who now want only what delights them most?

Suppose we pause upon this metaphysical point, divorced from reality though it is. It is thoroughly clarified by the following comparison. Imagine someone between two friends calling him, one from one direction and the other from another, but without using force to draw him; is it not clear that he is free to approach whichever of them he would like? Now imagine the same person, one of whose friends calls him without using any violence to draw him, while the other draws him with a chain of iron; is it not evident that he will follow the stronger? And lastly, imagine that each of the friends draws him to them with their own chain, but with different strength; is it not evident that he unfailingly follows the stronger? And if it happens that the efforts by which they respectively draw him are equally strong, then it is clear that he will not move in either direction.[24]

Imagine now that this same person is placed between the two friends, each restraining him with a chain out of fear that he will move further away; should we say that the person has recovered his former freedom and is in the same state he was before, balanced in choice? Is it not rather the case that he is unable to go one way or the other, that he cannot approach the one if the other's chain that holds him is not broken?

That, to some degree, is an image of the two freedoms; the first, Adam's, was unobstructedly balanced between opposites without being

24. The concluding clause of this sentence, *il est clair qu'il n'avancera d'aucun côté*, is not present in the manuscripts. Without it, the sentence is incomplete. This is an emendation with a long history, accepted by Mesnard, *Oeuvres*, 3:705, and Le Guern, *Oeuvres*, 2:273.

bound by either; but since becoming bound by concupiscence, he is beyond the condition of bringing himself to God unless the bond of God's grace draws him more strongly, breaking that of cupidity and making him say, *Lord, you have broken my bonds.*[25] If, then, that metaphysical position is right, and the good and the bad inclination bind him equally, who does not see that, very far from being in his initial state of balance, he is there less than ever; very far from being independent, he is entirely dependent; very far from being free, he is doubly a slave; and very far from being able to take himself in one direction or the other, he will remain immobile?

This comparison explains his condition relatively closely but not perfectly; that is because it is impossible to find in nature any example or comparison that conveys the actions of the will perfectly. There is this difference between free choice in the two conditions and the people in these two states: when they are bound in this way, although their bodies are bound their wills remain free, so that they are able to want to move themselves away from the one who draws them; but in the case of the freedom of those in the two conditions, the will itself is bound, and by delight. The comparison can only be just when the same chain that draws people in one direction has the strength to bring a victorious pleasure to their wills, which makes them love what draws them as unfailingly as the chain unfailingly draws their bodies; then, the body's immobility between the two chains that restrain it is a perfect image of the will's immobility between two equal delights.

To complete this comparison: as this person would not be returned to liberty by his opposed chains, and would only be so by the breaking of them, so we cannot be returned to balance by the equality of opposed inclinations; that could only be done by deliverance from the two inclinations; and as we are never delivered in this life from all concupiscence, it is clear from these principles that we cannot return to the unobstructed balance of our initial condition.

Hoc non est amplius in viribus,[26] etc.

25. Psalm 116:16.

26. "This is not fully within the powers [of free choice]"—Augustine, *De dono* 7.13 (also in §9, twice), from Sinnich, 183.

St. Augustine never meant that we are able to leave our sins and the inclination into which our corruption has precipitated us without being drawn by a more powerful delight, one not merely as strong but stronger and absolutely victorious; he shows this in all his writings.

You see by this how much this unobstructed ability is opposed both to the light of common sense and to the maxims of St. Augustine, as well as being so ridiculous in itself that it cannot be seriously proposed; for as we change from hour to hour, never remaining in the same state, it would follow that according to the measure of our attachment to or detachment from the things of the world, (which it is always within our ability to increase or decrease, even if not completely), this delight that belongs to grace, which would place us always within this unobstructed ability, would change from hour to hour in accord with our inconstancy, and (which would be monstrous for grace), it would increase and diminish in strength according to the measure of our attachment to and detachment from the world.

$9[1]

—

Once this difference[2] is properly understood, it is no longer surprising to see that St. Augustine says that the commandments are possible for us, and always so, not only for the righteous but for all, for salvation can only work with our cooperation: we do have the power to keep the commandments. That is because all these states of affairs find purchase in particularities, and there are not, among such statements, any applicable to particular individuals. But when we see in St. Augustine that we are unable to accomplish the commandments, and that grace alone brings about all salvation, that shows what his view is: those latter expressions are not opposed to the former because they are about different things.

What I say about St. Augustine should be applied to Scripture. All the expressions that indicate the necessity of cooperation, of the commandments, and of the corrections; and even the expressions: *if you want to, you will keep the commandments;*[3] *come to me all;*[4] and everything of that kind; *I anticipated the Lord,*[5] etc. *I have waited,*[6] *I have worked,*[7] etc.—these do not at all favor the semi-Pelagian error;

---

1. I translate §9 from Le Guern, *Oeuvres*, 2:275–83; see also Mesnard, *Oeuvres*, 3:663–77.

2. Presumably the difference between ability (*pouvoir*) and possibility (*possibilité*); or, perhaps that between general and particular effects, as discussed, by way of comment on Aquinas, in §1.

3. Matthew 19:17.

4. Matthew 11:28.

5. Psalm 119:147.

6. Psalm 40:2.

7. 1 Corinthians 15:10.

on the contrary, these passages: *he works the will and the action;*[8] *without me you can do nothing;*[9] *no one comes to me unless the Father wills it;*[10] *it is neither the one who acts nor the one who runs;*[11] etc.—and all those of that kind, found in such numbers, bring the semi-Pelagian error to ruin. The former passages are equivocal, the latter univocal.

All these expressions are no more contrary in Scripture than in St. Augustine, because they have to do with different objects. For you know that contrariety of propositions lies in their meaning rather than in their words. Otherwise, Scripture would be full of contradictions, as when it is said, *the Father is greater than me,*[12] and when it is said elsewhere that *Jesus Christ is equal to God;*[13] *if I glorify myself;*[14] etc. *So that I glorify myself,*[15] etc. And: *we are rectified by faith without works.*[16] And: *faith without works is dead.*[17] And all the others of this kind.

You well understand, then, how it is possible to say without contradiction that God anticipates us and that we anticipate God:[18] that *the commandments are always possible for the righteous,* and that *some commandments are sometimes not possible for some among the righteous;*[19] that *God does not leave the righteous, if the righteous do not leave,*[20] and *that God leaves the righteous first.*[21] All these states of affairs can obtain together because of difference in the topics they treat, and that

8. Philippians 2:13.

9. John 15:5.

10. John 6:44.

11. Romans 9:16.

12. John 14:28.

13. Philippians 2:6.

14. John 8:54.

15. 2 Thessalonians 1:4.

16. Romans 3:28.

17. James 2:26.

18. Augustine, *Enchiridion* 32.121 (also in §12, and again later in §9), perhaps from Sinnich, 389. Le Guern, *Oeuvres,* 2:276, does not italicize this sentence, even though it seems to be a quotation or allusion like the others in this and the preceding paragraph.

19. These two formulations refer to Pascal's distillation of the eleventh chapter of Trent's Decree on Rectification.

20. Prosper, *Ad capitula* 14, from Bourzeis, *Lettre,* 15–16.

21. Perhaps also an echo of Prosper, *Ad capitula* 14, as immediately above.

is what I will get you to see in St. Augustine and the Fathers by way of the few passages I present.

(Augustine, *Enchir.*, chap. 32) *Because we cannot believe in, hope for, or love God without willing to, nor arrive at heaven without willingly running there, how is it that it is not "by the one who wills or the one who runs but by God, who has mercy" unless "because that will is prepared by the Lord"? For otherwise, if it were by both, as if it had been said that our wills do not suffice if God does not have mercy, then also God's mercy would not suffice if we did not also will. And consequently, it would be just as possible to say: "It is not by God who has mercy, but by we who will, because God's mercy alone cannot accomplish it." If, perhaps, no Christian dares to say that, it remains possible to understand what has been said, "it is not by the one who wills or the one who runs but by God, who has mercy," so that everything is given by God who prepares our wills so as then to help them, and who offers them help after having prepared them. For our good will precedes many of God's gifts, though not all; and it is itself among those it does not in any way precede. In Scripture, we read both: "his mercy precedes me," and, "his mercy follows me." It precedes those who do not will so that they might come to do so; and it follows those who do will, so that they might not do so in vain.*[22]

(Augustine, *De gratia et lib. arbitr.*, chap. 17) *For it is God who works initially so that we might will, and who cooperates with those who will so that their work is brought to completion. That is why the Apostle said: "I am certain that the one who works this good work in you will bring it to completion by the day of Jesus Christ." And so, it is the same one who works independently of us so that we might will; and when we will in such a way as to prompt action, he cooperates with us.*[23]

(St. Fulgentius, l.1 *Ad Monim.*, ch. 14) *"I will make it so that you will walk in my righteousness and keep my commandments." What is it to say, "I will make it so that you will," except "all the good you will do will be by my work"? Therefore, he acts so that we might act; by this work in us is*

---

22. Augustine, *Enchiridion* 32.121 (also in §12, and again earlier in §9), from Sinnich, 389; Augustine quotes from Proverbs 8:35, Romans 9:16, Psalm 59:11, and Psalm 23:6.

23. Augustine, *De gratia et libero arbitrio* 17.33, from Sinnich, 389–90; Augustine quotes Philippians 1:6.

done all the good we do, of which it is said in Hebrews: "He disposes you toward all good, doing in you all that is pleasing to him."[24]

(Augustine, l. 1, *Retract.*, ch. 10) *I said: "That light does not nourish the eyes of brute beasts but the pure hearts of those who believe in God and have been converted from the love of visible and temporal things to keeping God's commandments, which each of us is able to do if we will to."* Never have the Pelagians said anything stronger, and yet St. Augustine, in retracting these words, did not find them absolutely incompatible with holy doctrine, adding to them simply these words: *The new Pelagians ought not think that this passage supports them. It is entirely true that each of us can do this if we will to, but the will is prepared by the Lord and then augmented by the gift of love so that we can. I did not say so in this passage because doing so was not necessary to the question.* What force would one grant to St. Augustine's first passage if he had not himself retracted it? And yet, who does not see that the following words are common to both parties: *each of us is able to keep the commandments if we will to?* What distinguishes the parties, though, is this: *the will is given by the Lord, and the gift of love makes the commandments possible.*[25]

This additional passage is of the same kind:

(Idem, chap. 22) *I said in another passage: "We cannot do what is good if we do not alter our wills; the Lord teaches this to be within our power: when you make the tree good, its fruit will also be good; when you make the tree bad, its fruit will also be bad." This passage is not at all against God's grace as we understand it, for we have the power to change our wills for the better; but that power is nothing if not given by God. We have power to do something if we do it when we will to, and there is nothing so much in our power as to will; but the will is prepared by the Lord, and that is how he gives it the power. That is how what I said next should be understood: "We have power to merit God's bounty or God's anger." For nothing is within our power except what comes from our wills,*

---

24. Fulgentius, *Ad Monimum* 2.14, from Sinnich, 390; Fulgentius quotes Ezekiel 36:27 and Hebrews 13:21.

25. The quotations in this paragraph are from Augustine, *Retractationes* 1.10.2 (also in §5), from Sinnich, 246; Augustine quotes his own *De Genesi* 1.3.6 (also in §12), and echoes Proverbs 8:35.

and when God makes them strong and powerful, good actions otherwise difficult or even impossible become easy.[26]

That is how it is possible to be both Catholic and Pelagian in saying that we are able to change our wills for the better; but Pelagians think that power ours, while Catholics think it God's and that something is possible for us only when God accords us a strong and powerful will, and impossible when he does not.

I wanted to report to you these important passages from St. Augustine, which seem so strongly to favor the Pelagians, so that you might not be at all surprised at certain passages, without comparison lesser, of which your brief paper[27] is full—*God does not command the impossible,*[28] and the like.

I come now to the question of most concern. I want to make you see that in St. Augustine's doctrine the commandments are sometimes impossible for some among the righteous; that as it is necessary always to ask for grace in order to get it, there are two perseverances to consider, one in prayer and the other in love, and because of that God gives two helps, one for perseverance in prayer and the other for perseverance in works; that it is also true that God never refuses help with works to those who do not stop asking for it, and in that sense God does not leave the righteous who do not leave him; but that it is also the case that God does not always give help in praying, and in that sense God leaves the righteous before the righteous leave him—this desertion always occurs in such a way that first God leaves us without the help necessary for prayer, then we cease praying, and then God leaves those among us who no longer pray.

This double desertion has been so well treated in the *Letter of an Abbé to a President,*[29] that it would be ridiculous to say more about it, and I do so only because you want it. Some proofs with respect to this matter:

---

26. Augustine, *Retractationes* 1.22.4 (also in §§1, 5, 12), from Sinnich, 246–47; Augustine quotes his own *Contra Adimantum* 26 (also in §§1, 5, 12), and echoes Matthew 12:33.

27. Presumably the imagined letter of Pascal's imagined interlocutor.

28. Probably Augustine, *De natura* 69.83 (also in §§1, 10, 14, 15), from Sinnich, 177.

29. Bourzeis, *Lettre.*

(Augustine, *De corr. et grat.*, chap. 12) St. Augustine, speaking of the reprobate who have entered into righteousness and who do not persevere in it, says: *They receive grace, but only for a time; they leave and are left, for they have been abandoned to their free choice by a righteous but hidden judgment.*[30] You see in these few words the double desertion I speak of. *They leave*, he says, *and are left*; in this desertion we precede, and God follows; there is no mystery in this desertion, but if one wants to know the reason why, etc.

We see the same thing in the reason St. Augustine supplies about the desertion of the righteous; for if he had established everywhere that falling again is permitted in order to show the righteous that they should hope only in God, is it not apparent that there is nothing so contrary to this need as to assure them that they always have unobstructed ability to pray, and that prayer is always certain to get what it asks for?

But if one wants to know the cause for which they are left, Augustine gives as the single reason that God has left them to their free choice. And if one asks why, their righteousness and that of the elect being the same, God leaves them, but not the elect, to their free choice, he says that it is by a hidden judgment. From which it is evident that it is neither because of bad use of the grace they had, nor because the effect of grace is ascribed to them, for in that case the distinction would not have been hidden, but, rather, well known. Finally, it is not for any reason that can be known by us; it comes by an occluded judgment—one of a strength which cannot be exaggerated. And since St. Augustine speaks in that place about all the reprobate who have grace for a time, it is evident from the understanding he provides of the matter how their fall happens.

This double desertion appears in all the writings of the saints, though more clearly in some than in others; it is very lucidly explained by St. Prosper when he says, *God does not leave any among the righteous who do not leave him first.* He adds, *and very often God makes it so that the righteous do not leave him.* From this you see that God does not always make it so that the righteous do not leave him. But if you ask St. Prosper why God makes it so that some but not others among

30. Augustine, *De correptione et gratia* 13.42 (also in §§8, 12), from Bourzeis, *Lettre*, 29.

the righteous do not leave him, he replies that the question, *why God retains these and not those is a question whose investigation is forbidden and whose answer is impossible to discover*; about this it is necessary to exclaim, *O profundity, O grandeur!*, etc.[31]

You see here the double desertion I speak of. Even in the absence of these passages, and all the others in which this is spoken of lucidly, the matter would not cease to be clear and to be absolutely necessary in its ordering principle. For who does not know that it is a principle beyond doubt in St. Augustine's doctrine that the reason for which one of two righteous people perseveres and the other does not is an absolutely incomprehensible secret? From which it is apparent that not all the righteous have unobstructed means for perseverance, because if the different uses to which their free choice put that ability were the cause of the difference between them, there would be no mystery.

Who does not know that in St. Augustine all the elect, which is to say all who persevere, do so by a grace that invincibly makes it so that they do, and without which they would not be able to?

Who does not know the difference St. Augustine places between the perseverance of Adam, that of the angels, and that of people now?

Who does not know that it is God who gives perseverance in prayer?

That grace makes itself desired and works in us all the good we do?

That the righteous are kept in that life of grace for as long as grace renders their will good, and are removed from it when their will becomes wicked?

And that, by contrast, the reprobate who are righteous are left in that life until their will alters, although they would have been able to be removed from it before that?

Who does not see in all these principles the falsehood of the proposition that the righteous always have unobstructed ability to persevere, at least in prayer? For if that is so, and ability is unobstructed and not like the sanctifying grace of the Thomists[32] whose effects are never unobstructed, it follows that even the reprobate righteous are able to

---

31. The italicized passages in this paragraph are from Prosper, *Ad capitula* 14, from Bourzeis, *Lettre*, 16, except for the concluding phrase, which is from Romans 11:33.

32. Pascal probably has in mind Thomas, *Summa Theologiae* 1–2.109.9, corpus (also in §§5, 8), although his immediate source remains unclear.

persevere; also that there is no difference between Adam's perseverance, that of the angels, and that of the present day; that there is no further mystery in the distinction of those who persevere from those who do not; and finally, all the absurdities contrary to the main points of the doctrine of the doctor of grace.

Because the passages in which St. Augustine establishes all these points are perhaps not familiar to you, I provide those I have to hand:

(St. Augustine, l. 2 *De peccator. merit.*, chap. 17) *It follows that each of us sometimes knows to undertake, to continue, and to accomplish a good work, and sometimes does not know; sometimes we take delight in it and sometimes not, so that we learn that it is not by our power but by God's gift that we know and experience delight, and in that way are healed of pride; and we know how truly it is said that the Lord will give delight and the earth that we are will bear fruit.*[33] Is it not evident that in this passage St. Augustine establishes the powerlessness we find in ourselves to complete some good work by saying that delight in it is not always with us so that we learn not to aggrandize ourselves—which would not be so, had we unobstructed ability to accomplish good work?

(St. Augustine, *ibid.*, chap. 19) *This is why God waits to heal even his saints and faithful of some vices, so that the delight they have in what is good is less than sufficient entirely to accomplish righteousness.* And then: *in doing this, God wills us not to damn ourselves, but to become humble.*[34] Is it not clear that this plan of God's work would not work for the saints if they had unobstructed ability to accomplish righteousness?

(Fulgentius, l. 1 *De veritate praedestin.*, chap. 15 and 16) Consider also the force of these passages: *The grace that God gives to the vessels of mercy begins with the heart's illumination; it does not find our wills good, but rather renders them good; that same grace first elects them so that they become elect, and that graceful choice is neither received nor loved if that same grace does not work that effect in our hearts. And so the reception of and desire for that grace is the work of the same grace.* And then: *therefore, grace itself first brings about understanding, love,*

---

33. Augustine, *De peccatorum meritis* 2.17.27 (also in §§6, 13), from Sinnich, 112–13; Augustine alludes to Psalm 85:13.

34. Augustine, *De peccatorum meritis* 2.19.33 (also in §§6,13), from Sinnich, 113.

and desire.[35] Therefore, either the ability the righteous always have to desire grace is only sufficient and not unobstructed, like that of the Thomists; or, if it is unobstructed, they are able to love grace without it bringing about that result in them. But that latter point is so contrary to this saint's principles that we conclude that because grace is never received or desired except when it itself brings about that result, it is not the case that the righteous have unobstructed ability by means of which their free choice might itself bring about that result. I cannot emphasize this enough.

(Fulgentius, l. 2, *De verit. praedest.*, chap. 4) *When, therefore, God commanded us to will what is good, our need was shown to us; but because we are not capable of this ourselves, we were advised to ask help from the one who gave us the precept. We are, however, unable to ask unless God brings it about in us that we will to do so.*[36] He does not say that we do not ask it if God does not bring it about, but that we are unable to ask it if God does not bring about in us exactly the will to ask it. Following St. Fulgentius, there is therefore no unobstructed ability to ask for the accomplishment of the precepts on the part of those who lack will to do so; and further following him, ability and will are so connected that we never have ability if God does not give us will.

(Fulgentius, *Epist.* 4, chap. 2) *Who among us can pray as we should if the divine doctor does not himself breathe into us the beginnings of that desire; or, who among us can persevere in prayer if God does not augment in us what he has begun, does not nourish what he has sown, and does not bring to perfection by the result of his mercy what he has given freely to the unworthy by his prevenient mercy?*[37] Therefore, we lack the ability to persevere in prayer, if God does not make it so that we persevere.

(St. Augustine, *De dono persever.*, chap. 23) *They do not want to understand that when we pray it is God's gift.*[38]

(idem, *In Psal.* 118, consi. 14) *It is he who makes us ask for what we want to get, look for what we want to find, and knock.* And then: *it is the*

---

35. Fulgentius, *De veritate praedestinationis* 1.15.33–1.16.34, from Sinnich, 160.

36. Fulgentius, *De veritate praedestinationis* 2.4.6 (also in §§8, 10), from Sinnich, 178.

37. Fulgentius, *Epistulae* 4.2, from Sinnich, 436.

38. Augustine, *De dono* 23.64 (also in §8), from Sinnich, 438.

spirit of God dwelling in us that makes it so that we cry out.[39] Therefore it is not by unobstructed ability that we ask or pray.

(Augustine, *Epist.* 105) *Prayer itself is among God's gifts.*[40]

(Fulgentius, l. 1 *De verit. praedest.*, chap. 18) *Therefore, so that we will to believe in God, he has given us that good will; so that we actually do believe, he has given us faith; so that we might love him, he has given us the grace of love.* And then: *and so, it is grace alone that brings about good will in us. It alone gives faith to that will, and when that good will has received faith, it begins to do good so long as it does not lack grace; for grace brings about good will in us.*[41]

(St. Augustine, l. *de dono persever.*, chap. 7) *So that we might not distance ourselves from God, our doing so is given to us only by God. It is now no longer among the strengths of free choice.* And then: *God willed that after our fall, it would no longer belong to us either to approach him or depart from him apart from his grace.*[42]

(Augustine, *De grat. et lib.*, chap. 15 and 16) *By grace, we are made so that we have good will in place of the wicked will we had. By grace, the good will now begun in us is augmented so that it becomes sufficiently great.*[43]

---

39. Augustine, *Enarrationes* 118.14.2 (also in §8), from Sinnich, 438.

40. Augustine, *Epistulae* 194.4.16 (also in §8), from Sinnich, 438.

41. Fulgentius, *De veritate pradestinationis* 1.18.38 (also in §8), from Sinnich, 490.

42. Augustine, *De dono* 7.13 (also in §8, and earlier in §9), from Sinnich, *Trias*,183.

43. Augustine, *De gratia et libero arbitrio* 15.31 (also in §1), from Sinnich, 180.

$10[1]

—

St. Augustine, and the Fathers who followed him, spoke of the commandments only to say that they are not impossible for love, and that they are made for us only to make us aware of the need we have for love, which is the only thing that accomplishes them.

(Augustine, *De nat. et grat.*, chap. 69) *A righteous and good God is unable to command the impossible; this indicates to us that we should do what is easy and ask help with what is difficult—for everything is easy for love.*[2] And elsewhere: (*De Perfect. justit.*,[3] chap. 10) *Who does not know that what is done by love is not difficult? There are those who resent the pain of accomplishing the precepts, and who force themselves to observe them out of fear; perfect love, however, casts out fear and renders easy the precepts' yoke; very far from crushing us by its weight, that yoke lifts us up as with wings. And that love does not come from our free choice if the grace of Jesus Christ does not help us; that is because it is infused in our hearts, not by ourselves but by the Holy Spirit. And Scripture indicates to us that the precepts are not difficult for a single reason: so that the soul resenting their weight understands that it has not yet received the strength by which the precepts become easy and light.*[4] And so on.

(Fulgentius l. 2 *De verit. praedest.*, chap. 4) *When we are commanded*

1. I translate $10 from Le Guern, *Oeuvres*, 2:283–87; see also Mesnard, *Oeuvres*, 3:642–48.

2. Augustine, *De natura* 69.83 (also in §§1, 9, 14, 15), from Sinnich, 177.

3. Le Guern, *Oeuvres*, 2:293, uppercases the initial p of the text's title without comment, though elsewhere in his edition it is lowercased. Mesnard, *Oeuvres*, 3:642, lowercases.

4. Augustine, *De perfectione* 10.21 (also in §§1, 14), from Sinnich, 177–78; Augustine quotes 1 John 4:18 and Romans 5:5.

to will, our need is indicated to us; because we are not capable of this our-selves, we are shown from whom we should ask it; but, however, we are always unable to make that request if God does not work that will in us.[5]

(Prosper, *Epist. ad Demetriad.*) *The precepts are given to us for only one reason: to make us look for help from the one who commands us.* And so on.[6]

(Augustine, *De nat. et grat.*, chap. 15 and 16) *The Pelagians imagine that they say something important when they say that God would not command something we are not able to do. Who does not know that? But God does command things we are unable to do, so that we might under-stand from whom we should ask them.*[7]

(Augustine, *De corrept. et grat.*, chap. 3) *Reader, recognize in the precept what you should do, recognize in the correction that it is your lack that you fail to do it, and recognize in prayer from where you can get the ability to do it.*[8]

(Augustine, *De perfect. justit. respon. ad ratiocin.*, xi, chap. 5) *The law commands so that we may realize that we lack strength to accomplish it and not inflate ourselves with pride, but, being fatigued, have recourse to grace; in that way the law, shocking us, leads us to the love of Jesus Christ.*[9]

(Augustine, *De perfect. justit.*, chap. 10) St. Augustine attributes an objection to Celestius,[10] namely: *The commandments are not impossi-ble, but on the contrary easy. Deuteronomy says: "And God will turn to eat with you as he did with your fathers if you listen to the voice of the Lord, your God, to keep and do all his commandments and judgments, and his commandments written in the book of his law; if you turn toward the Lord your God with all your heart and soul. For the commandment I give you today is neither heavy nor far from you. It is not in heav-en, so that you might say, 'Who will go up to heaven and call us to go*

---

5. Fulgentius, *De veritate praedestinationis* 2.4.6 (also in §§8, 9), from Sinnich, 178.

6. Prosper, *Epistula ad Demetriadem* 15 (also in §14), from Sinnich, 179.

7. Augustine, *De gratia et libero arbitrio* 16.32 (also in §§2, 12), from Sinnich, 180. Sinnich's location of this excerpt is correct; Pascal's is in error.

8. Augustine, *De correptione* 3.5, from Sinnich, 178.

9. Augustine, *De perfectione* 5.11, from Sinnich, 182.

10. Celestius (fifth century) was an associate of Pelagius; his views were criticized by Augustine (as here) and condemned at Ephesus in 431.

there, so that we may do it? It is not at the bottom of the sea, so that you might say, 'Who will go there to bring it to us?' For the word is close to you and in your mouth so that you may do it, and in your heart and hands." Similarly, the Lord says in the Gospel: "Come to me you who are burdened and I will relieve you. Take my yoke upon yourself and learn from me that I am gentle and humble of heart and you will find repose for your souls, for my yoke is easy and my burden light." Similarly, in the Letter of St. John, "It is the love of God that you will keep the command-ments, and they are not heavy." On this, St. Augustine comments: *After hearing these legitimate evangelical and apostolic testimonies, be edified by them about grace; those ignorant of God's righteousness do not hear them, and, wanting to establish righteousness for themselves, have not submitted to God's righteousness. For if they have not heard what's said in Deuteronomy as St. Paul says, so that they believe in righteousness with their hearts and confess with their mouths that they are saved, because those who are healthy have no need of medicine, but rather the sick,*[11] *they should at least be warned by the passage from St. John, cited last, that God's commandments are neither difficult nor heavy for God's love, which is scattered in our hearts by none other than the Holy Spirit.*[12]

It would be useless to report more passages on this topic. We need no more than a sketch of this Father's principles to know that when he says the commandments are not impossible, he intends it in the sense that they are not impossible for love, which can be scattered in the heart by the Holy Spirit; this against the claim of his adversaries that the commandments are not impossible for us in another sense, namely that we always have strength to accomplish them, or to ask for the means to do so in the next moment.

I think that this suffices to get you to see that the Council estab-lished the possibility of the commandments only in the sense that they are not impossible for love, which is evident in the Council's preferred language, its proof, its conclusion, its canons, and in the sense that

11. Le Guern, *Oeuvres*, 2:285, provides a period here. A comma makes an altogether more sensible sentence. See Mesnard, *Oeuvres*, 3:645.

12. Augustine, *De perfectione* 10.22, from Sinnich, 272–73; Augustine quotes or echoes (or has Celestius quote or echo) in order: Deuteronomy 30:9–14, Matthew 11:28, 1 John 5:3, Romans 10:10, Matthew 9:12.

St. Augustine himself gives to his preferred language, which the Council has only repeated in the same sense. It now remains to consider the sense of the Council concerning the possibility of the commandments in the future, and the view of the remainder of the Pelagians[13] on this same subject.

To say no more than what is necessary, it suffices to cite canon twenty-two of the Council, which anathematizes those who say that the righteous are able to persevere without God's special help; but because I want to treat this same material in such a way that you have no remaining scruple about it, I will say some more.

Observe, therefore, that all the following questions are one and the same.

1.[14] Whether all the righteous, at the first moment of their righteousness, have unobstructed ability to accomplish the precepts in the immediately following moment?

Whether all the righteous, at the first moment of their righteousness, have unobstructed ability to persevere in it (for to accomplish the commandments in the future and to persevere in them are one and the same)?

This question, too, is the same: whether the righteous, while they are righteous, are able to persevere in prayer and in desire for it unobstructedly in the next moment—(for if they are able to persevere in asking for righteousness, they are also able to persevere in righteousness itself; for by the Gospel's promises, grace unfailingly gives what is asked for, and since one of the propositions is anathematized by the Council of Trent,[15] it is evident that the other also is.)?

This question, too, is not different from the preceding ones:

Whether God ever leaves any among the righteous without the grace necessary to pray in the following moment without those righteous having previously left God by way of some sin, even a venial one?

---

13. For the meaning of the phrase *les restes des Pélagiens* see notes to §1.

14. Pascal appears to have begun to enumerate the questions with which §10 ends, but not to have carried the plan through.

15. That is, the proposition that the righteous are able to persevere without special help, which is anathematized in canon twenty-two.

For if God never refuses the grace of prayer in the immediately following moment to the righteous who have not yet sinned, it is evident that it can be said of all the righteous that they are able to persevere in prayer because God always gives them grace unobstructedly sufficient for future prayer, and so, by the Gospel's promises, they will always get the results of their prayer. Because ability to persevere in prayer implies ability to persevere in righteousness, each of the righteous is able to persevere in righteousness without special help, but rather by way of help common to all the righteous—which directly contradicts the Council. And it is not possible to escape this by saying that it is morally impossible that the righteous persevere without venial sin, and lose this ability when they sin venially, and that consequently they will not persevere without special help. That muddle is useless, for the Council anathematizes not only those who say that the righteous persevere in righteousness without special help, but also those who say that the righteous are able to persevere in righteousness without special help. Consequently, the Council also anathematizes that latter proposition.

§11[1]

≈

St. Augustine's Doctrine

St. Augustine distinguishes two states of human beings, before and after sin, and has two sets of views appropriate to these two states.

Before Adam's Sin

God created the first of us, and in him the entirety of human nature.
He created him righteous, healthy, and strong;
Without concupiscence;
With free choice equally flexible toward good and evil;
Desiring beatitude and unable not to desire it.
God could not create any of us with absolute will for damnation.
God did not create any of us with absolute will for salvation.
God created all of us, without exception, with the conditional will to save us should we keep his precepts.
If not, then to dispose himself toward us as master, which is to say, damning us or having mercy on us according to his good pleasure.
We were innocent from God's hands, strong, healthy, and just; and yet, we were not able to keep the commandments without God's grace.
God could not justly impose precepts upon Adam and upon the innocent without giving them grace necessary for their accomplishment.
If at our creation, we were without grace sufficient[2] and necessary

1. I translate §11 from Le Guern, *Oeuvres*, 2:287–93; see also Mesnard, *Oeuvres*, 3:792–99; Levi & Levi, 220–26, provides a complete English rendering of §11; Miel, 203–7, renders about one-half of it into English.

2. See the discussion of the meaning of *suffisant* in the interpretive essay following the translation.

for accomplishing the precepts, we would not have sinned by transgressing them.

God gave Adam sufficient grace, which is to say grace in addition to which nothing else was necessary for accomplishing the precepts and remaining in righteousness. By this means, Adam could persevere, or not, according to his good pleasure,

So that Adam's free choice could, as master of this sufficient grace, render it useless or effective, according to his own good pleasure.

God left and permitted Adam's free choice the good or evil use of that grace.

If Adam had used that grace to persevere, he would have merited glory, which is to say eternal confirmation in grace without danger of ever sinning; just as the good angels merited it by the merit of a similar grace.

And then, each of Adam's descendants would have been born in righteousness, and with sufficient grace like his by means of which they would have been able to persevere, or not, according to their good pleasure; and to merit eternal glory, or not, like Adam.

Adam, tempted by the Devil, succumbed, rebelled against God, infringed his precepts, and willed to be independent of and equal to God.

After Adam's Sin

Adam, having sinned and rendered himself worthy of eternal death,
As punishment for his rebellion,
God left him to creaturely love.
And his will, which before was not at all drawn to creatures by any concupiscence, became filled with concupiscence, sown there by the Devil, not by God.

Concupiscence then arose in his members; it titillated and delighted his will with evil; shadows filled his mind in such a way that his will, previously balanced between good and evil, without delight in or titillation by one or the other, but following, without any previously existing appetite on its part, what it took to be most appropriate to felicity, found itself now charmed by the concupiscence which had arisen in his members. And his mind, so strong, righteous, and clear, was obscured by ignorance.

This sin has passed from Adam to all his posterity, which has been corrupted in him like a fruit coming from a bad seed; all who come from Adam are born in ignorance and concupiscence, guilty of Adam's sin, worthy of eternal death.

Free choice remained flexible between good and evil, but with the difference that while in Adam, it was not at all titillated by evil and to move toward the good it had only to recognize it, it has now such a powerfully sweet delight in evil because of concupiscence that it unfailingly moves itself toward evil as if it were its good, choosing it voluntarily and quite freely and with joy, as that in which it senses its beatitude.

Each of us, belonging to this corrupt mass, is equally worthy of eternal death and God's anger; God was therefore able justly to abandon us all to damnation, without mercy.

Nevertheless, it pleased God to choose, elect, and separate from this equally corrupt mass, in which he could see only what merits evil, a number of people of every age, sex, condition, complexion, country, and time—that is, of all kinds.

God separated the elect from others for reasons unknown to angels or to us, by sheer mercy, in the absence of merit.

God's elect constitute a whole which is sometimes called *world* because it is scattered throughout the world; sometimes *all*, because it constitutes a totality; sometimes *many* because there are many of them; and sometimes *few* because there are few in proportion to the totality of the deserted.

The deserted constitute a totality called *world, all,* and *many*, but never *few*.

God, by absolute and irrevocable will, willed to save the elect by purely gratuitous bounty, and abandoned the others to their evil desires to which he could justly have abandoned everyone.

To save his elect, God sent Jesus Christ, to satisfy his righteousness and to merit by his mercy the grace of redemption—medicinal grace, the grace of Jesus Christ, which is nothing other than sweetness and delight in God's law scattered in the heart by the Holy Spirit; that sweetness not only equals but surpasses even the flesh's concupiscence; it fills the will with a greater delight in good than concupiscence offers it in evil; and in that way, free choice, charmed by the softnesses and the pleasures breathed into it by the Holy Spirit more than by sin's attractions, unfailingly chooses the law of God for the sole reason that it finds more satisfaction in it, and senses there its beatitude and its felicity.

The result is that those to whom it pleases God to give that grace unfailingly move themselves by their free choice to prefer God to creatures. That is why it can equally well be said that free choice moves itself by way of that grace, because in effect it does move itself; or that grace moves free choice, because whenever grace is given, free choice unfailingly follows.

Those to whom it pleases God to give this grace until the end of their lives persevere unfailingly in that preference, and choosing in that way by their own will until death to accomplish rather than to violate the law because they sense more satisfaction in it, they merit glory, both by the help of grace which has overcome their concupiscence, and by their own choice and the movement of their free choice which voluntarily and freely moves them accordingly.

All those to whom such grace is not given, or not given so that it lasts until the end of their lives, remain so titillated and charmed by their concupiscence that they unfailingly love to sin more than not to, because they find more satisfaction in it.

Dying in that way, in their sins, they merit eternal death because they have chosen evil by their own free choice.

This is how we are saved or damned, following God's pleasure in choosing us as recipients of grace from the corrupt mass to which he could justly abandon us all.

All are, for their part, equally guilty when God separates them.

Opinions of the Remainder of the Pelagians[3]

The remainder of the Pelagians easily agree with St. Augustine about the state of innocence: that God made us righteous with sufficient grace by which we could, if we willed, persevere, or not; that, at creation, God had a conditional will to save all of us so long as we put that grace to

---

3. For the meaning of the phrase *les restes des Pélagiens*, see notes to §1.

good use; that such use being left to his free choice, Adam sinned, and in him all human nature; that he was punished for concupiscence and ignorance; that all his posterity is born worthy of damnation, with the double curse of ignorance and concupiscence. In all these things they agree. But they differ about God's conduct toward us after sin. Here is what they think:

that God would have been unjust had he not willed to save all (in the corrupt mass), and had he not given help to all sufficient for salvation;

that God could not have avoided being invidious in separating the one from the other had they not, for their part, given some occasion for that separation;

that God could not, without wounding their free choice, will absolutely to make it so that they would accomplish the precepts by his grace.

On these foundations, they advance the claim that God had a general, equal, and conditional will to save all (in the corrupt mass), as at creation, so long as they willed to accomplish the precepts. And because they needed a new grace as a result of their sin, Jesus Christ became incarnate to merit for them, and to offer to all without a single exception and for the course of their lives without interruption, grace sufficient only to believe in and pray to God for help.

That those who do not make use of this grace, and who remain in their sins until death in spite of this help, are justly abandoned, punished, and damned by God.

That those who use this grace well, believing in and praying to God, give to God in doing those things occasion to separate them from the rest and to provide them other helps, which some call effective and others merely sufficient, for their salvation.

So that all those who use that general and sufficient grace well obtain from God's mercy graces to do good works and to arrive at salvation.

Those who do not make good use of that grace remain damned.

In this way, all are saved or damned according as it pleases them to render vain or effective the sufficient grace given to all for belief or prayer—God on his part having an equal will to save all.

Calvin's Opinion[4]

Calvin has no conformity with St. Augustine, differing with him in everything, from beginning to end.

He claims that God, having created Adam and all of us in him, had, in creating them, no conditional will to save them; that the end he had in mind when creating the most noble among his creatures had no ambiguity: he created some with absolute will to damn them, and others with absolute will to save them. That God decreed this for his glory. That therefore this decree is just, although it is not evident to us how, for all that gives God glory is just, since it is just that he has all glory.

That, nevertheless, God, unable by his righteousness to damn them without sin, did not permit, but rather decreed and ordained, Adam's sin. That Adam, having sinned necessarily by God's decree, became worthy of eternal death. That he lost his free choice. That he no longer had any possibility of turning toward good, even with the most effective grace.

That Adam's sin was communicated to all his posterity, not naturally, as a defect in seeds is transmitted to their fruit, but by God's decree, according to which all are born guilty of the sin of their first father, without free choice, without possibility of turning toward good even with effective grace, and worthy of eternal death.

That all being guilty, God disposed himself toward them as master. That he willed to save only those he created to save. That he willed to damn those he created to damn. That for this outcome, Jesus Christ became incarnate in order to merit the salvation of those chosen from the yet-innocent mass before foreknowledge of sin.

That God gives to those, and only to them, the grace of Jesus Christ, which they never lose after receiving it, and which moves their will toward the good (not that it makes it so that the will moves itself there, but that grace does the moving in spite of the will's opposition)—like a stone, like a saw, like something dead to action, without capacity to move itself with grace and to cooperate with grace, because free choice is lost and entirely dead.

4. Pascal's principal source for this discussion of the Calvinists is Bourzeis, *Saint Augustin victorieux*, 108–44.

Accordingly, that grace works alone; and although it remains and works good works until death, it is not free choice that does them or moves itself by its choice; on the contrary, while grace works good works in it, it merits eternal death. Jesus Christ alone is meritorious; the righteous are in no way so; Jesus Christ's merits are only imputed and applied to them, and the righteous are in that way saved by Christ's merits.

Accordingly, those to whom this grace is once given are unfailingly saved, not by their good works or good will, of which they have none, but by the merits of Jesus Christ, which are applied to them.

Those to whom this grace is not given are unfailingly damned because of the sins they commit by God's order and command, who inclines them thus for his glory.

Accordingly, all are saved or damned as it has pleased God to choose them in Adam at the point of their creation and to incline them to do good or evil for his glory.

All were, for their part, equally innocent when God separated them.

$$\S12^1$$

≈

One should say the same thing[2] to those who abuse St. Augustine's equivocal passages rather than explaining them by the univocal ones. I will not pause on the weak passages, such as, *we never precede God, and our good will precedes many of God's gifts*—for he explains it himself very clearly at the place from which those last words were taken.[3]

(Augustine, *Enchirid.*, chap. 32) *For our good will precedes many of God's gifts, though not all; and it is itself among those it does not in any way precede. In Scripture, we read both: "his mercy precedes me," and "his mercy follows me." It precedes those who do not will so that they might come to do so; and it follows those who do will, so that they might not do so in vain.*[4]

The true cause of all these different expressions is that all our good actions have two sources: our will, and God's. As St. Augustine says: *God does not save us without us;*[5] and, *if we so will, we can keep the commandments;*[6] and, *meriting and demeriting depend on the movement of our will.*[7] The upshot is that if we ask why adults are saved, we

1. I translate §12 from Le Guern, *Oeuvres*, 2:293–98; see also Mesnard, *Oeuvres*, 3:677–83; Miel, 207–8, renders about ten percent of §12 into English.

2. Perhaps a reference back to Prosper's statement about Augustine's equivocal and univocal passages quoted in §1.

3. Augustine, *Enchiridion* 32.121 (also in §9), from Sinnich, 389.

4. Augustine, *Enchiridion* 32.121 (also in §9), from Sinnich, 389; Augustine echoes Psalm 59:11 and Psalm 23:6.

5. Augustine, *Sermones* 169.11.13 (also in §7), from Sinnich, 429.

6. Perhaps Augustine, *De gratia et libero arbitrio* 16.32 (also in §§2, 10), from Sinnich, 431.

7. Perhaps an echo of Augustine, *Contra Adimantum* 26 (also in §§1, 5, 9), which

can rightly say that it is because they willed it so, and that it is because God willed it so. If one or the other had not so willed, it would not have happened. But even though these two causes have concurred to produce this result, there is nevertheless considerable difference in the concurrence of each; our will is not the cause of God's, while God's is the cause, source, and principle of ours, working that will in us. The result is that although we can attribute actions either to our will or to God's, and the two causes seem to concur equally, nevertheless there is this thoroughgoing difference: we can attribute an action solely to God's will to the exclusion of ours; but that action cannot be attributed solely to our wills to the exclusion of God's.

For when we say that an action comes from our will, we consider human will as the secondary cause, not as the primary cause; when we look for the primary cause, we attribute the action to God's will alone and exclude it from ours. Accordingly, St. Paul, having said, *I have worked more than anyone,* adds *not me,* which is to say, *I have not worked, but his grace, which is with me, has done so.*[8] This shows that he attributes his work to his own will, and that he refuses to do so, depending upon whether he looks for the secondary cause or the primary; but he never attributes it to himself alone, giving it instead to grace alone, and that it is when speaking correctly that he says he gives it to grace alone. In accord with this, he says: *I live, not me, but Jesus Christ in me.*[9] He says, *I live,* and adds, *I do not live.* It is true that life is his to the extent that he wants to mark the secondary cause, and that it is not his to the extent that he wants to mark the primary cause. But to speak correctly, he attributes that life to Jesus Christ and never to himself alone.

This is the origin of all the apparent contrarieties that the Word's incarnation, which joined God to us as power to weakness, has placed within the works of grace.

You should not be surprised after this to see in St. Augustine the

---

Pascal quotes elsewhere only as it occurs in *Retractationes* 1.22.4; in those places, he takes the text from Sinnich, 246–47.

8. 1 Corinthians 15:10.

9. Galatians 2:20.

same contrarieties as in Scripture. I will point out to you only one or two of the principal places,[10] such as this: *This light does not nourish the eyes of brute beasts, but the pure hearts of those who believe in God and who have turned from the love of visible things to the accomplishment of the precepts: which all of us can do if we will.*[11]

Who does not believe that in this St. Augustine and Pelagius agree? For that heretic never said anything more formal in support of the forces of freedom. However, St. Augustine finds this expression sufficiently equivocal that he takes it to be capable of a sense entirely contrary to what it claims; because it is also capable of a bad sense, he retracts and retouches it in this way in his *Retractations* (chap. 10): *The new Pelagians ought not think that this passage supports them; it is entirely true that each of us can do this if we will to, but the will is prepared by the Lord and then augmented by the gift of love so that we can; I did not say so in this passage because doing so was not necessary to the question.*[12] From this we can see at once that, when expressions of this kind escape St. Augustine on occasions when it is not necessary to explicate them, it is ridiculous to turn these equivocal terms toward a sense entirely contrary to their principles; and we can see at root that the Catholic sense of the words, *we can keep the commandments if we will* is that we are given that ability by the gift of love.

This other place is of the same kind: *None can do good who do not change their will, something the Lord teaches to be within our power when he says, "When the tree is good, so is its fruit; when the tree is bad, so is its fruit."*[13]

Here are some expressions it is necessary to take from St. Augustine if one wants to accuse him of contradiction, and not of that alone: *the commandments are possible for the righteous.*[14] And yet, who does not

10. *Endroits* is a conjectural emendation accepted by almost all editors: Le Guern, *Oeuvres*, 2:295; Mesnard, *Oeuvres*, 3:679.

11. Augustine, *De Genesi* 1.3.6 (also in §9), probably from Sinnich, 246, where it occurs within Augustine, *Retractationes* 1.10.2 (also in §§5, 9)

12. Augustine, *Retractationes* 1.10.2 (also in §§5, 9), from Sinnich, 246; Augustine echoes Proverbs 8:35.

13. Augustine, *Contra Adimantum* 26, probably from Sinnich, 246, where it occurs within Augustine, *Retractationes* 1.22.4 (also in §§1, 5, 9); Augustine quotes Matthew 7:17.

14. Pascal's distillation of the eleventh chapter of Trent's Decree on Rectification.

see that the word *power* is imprecise enough to contain all kinds of opinions? It is a very natural and familiar way of talking to say of something that it is *within our power* and mean that we do it when we will; then does it not follow that we have the ability in this sense to keep the commandments and to alter our wills, so that as soon as we will to do so not only does it happen but there is a contradiction if it does not? But if we say of something that *we are able to do it* only so long as it is within the ability we call *unobstructed*, which is also a very ordinary way to use the word *ability*, then in this sense we no longer have such an ability except when it is given to us by God. This expression of St. Augustine is Catholic in the first sense, and Pelagian in the second. St. Augustine speaks of these matters in this way in his *Retractations* (liv. 1, chap. 22): *This passage is not at all against God's grace as we understand it, for we have power to change our wills for the better. But that power is nothing if not given by God. For we have power to do something if we do it when we will to, and nothing is so much within our power as our will. But the will is prepared by the Lord. It is in that way that he gives us power to will. That is how what I said next is to be understood: "It is within our power to merit reward or pain." For we have power to do nothing except what comes from our wills, and when God makes them strong and powerful good actions that were previously difficult or even impossible become easy.*[15]

After such strong examples, you cannot doubt that any semi-Pelagian proposition can also be Augustinian.

Accordingly, St. Augustine does not contradict himself when, having written two entire books[16] to show that perseverance is God's gift, he does not avoid saying in one place in his books that perseverance can be merited by prayer; for it is beyond doubt that perseverance in righteousness can be merited by perseverance in prayer, but not the

---

15. Augustine, *Retractationes* 1.22.4 (also in §§1, 5, 9), from Sinnich, 246–47; Augustine quotes his own *Contra Adimantum* 26 (also in §§1, 5, 9); there are also echoes of Matthew 12:33.

16. That is, presumably, *De dono* and *De praedestinatione*. Pascal's way of putting things here suggests knowledge of these books as a whole rather than only by way of excerpts in florilegia such as Sinnich; but all his excerpts from these two books are in fact taken from there.

other way around—and it is properly perseverance in prayer which is the special gift of God of which the Council of Trent speaks; it is in this way that perseverance in general is a special gift, and perseverance that can be merited is perseverance in works. This is evident in the very expression under discussion: *perseverance can be merited by prayer.*[17]

Accordingly, St. Augustine does not contradict himself when, having established by all his principles that grace is so effective and so necessary that we never leave God if God has not first left us without this help, so that, for as long as it pleases God to retain us, we never separate ourselves from him, he does not avoid saying in some places that God does not leave those among the righteous who have not left him; these two states of affairs subsist together because of their different senses. For God does not cease giving help to those who do not cease asking for it. But also, we would not cease asking for it if God had not ceased giving us grace to ask for it, so that, with respect to this double cessation, God always commences one, and never the other.

This double desertion, one in which God commences and the other in which God follows, is clearly indicated to you by St. Prosper, when he says, *God does not leave if not left, and God very often makes it so that he is not left. But how is it that he retains some and not others? It is neither permissible to look for nor possible to find the answer to that.*[18] The truth that God does not leave if not left shows the desertion that we commence. *And God very often makes it so that he is not left*—therefore, God does not always do this. And when God is left, it is because he does not make it so that he is not, because he does not retain—and so the first conclusion is that God does not retain, and is then left, because those he retains do not leave him; is that not exactly what I say? The first desertion consists in God's not retaining, following which we leave; this gives way to the second desertion, in which God leaves. In one of these desertions, God follows: no mystery there, for there is nothing strange in God leaving those who have left him. But the first desertion is entirely mysterious and incomprehensible.

St. Augustine, too, Prosper's master, treats the same thing with the same clarity when, in discussing generally the fall of all the reprobate

---

17. Augustine, *De dono* 6.10, from Sinnich, 683.
18. Prosper, *Ad capitula* 14, from Bourzeis, *Lettre*, 15–16.

who came to righteousness for a time, he says that *they receive grace for a time; they leave and are left; for they have been abandoned to their free choice by a righteous but hidden judgment*—from this it is evident that we leave and then are left; that is the desertion in which God follows, in which there is nothing mysterious. But if we ask why they leave, St. Augustine gives the reason that *they have been abandoned to their free choice.* They are, therefore, abandoned before leaving, and, further, they leave only because they are left. That is the desertion that God commences, and it is done by a hidden and impenetrable judgment.[19]

It seems, therefore, that God leaves only because he is left, and that we leave only because we are left; it is therefore absurd to conclude that, according to St. Augustine's views, God never leaves first because he has said that God does not leave first; and that both together are true: God does and does not leave first, because of the two different ways of leaving.

There is no need of anything more to make you see how to bring these apparent contradictions to agreement. I will not, therefore, extend myself further on the subject. But because I have been gradually led to speak of the desertion of the righteous, and because I know that to be the one difficulty that remains for you, and the one topic among all those contested at the moment that you have difficulty in believing to be St. Augustine's, I will not end this letter without fully clarifying this point to you, if God permits.

I want, then, to get you to see, with St. Augustine, that the righteous would never leave God if God had not left them by not giving them all the grace necessary to persevere in prayer; and that not only is this a point of the theology of that Father, but that it cannot be denied without destroying every principle and foundation of his doctrine, and without falling into the wanderings of his adversaries and of the enemies of grace against whom he fought and won throughout his life with these same writings, by which the Church fights them and will always win.

---

19. The quotations in this paragraph are from Augustine, *De correptione* 13.42 (also in §§8, 9), from Bourzeis, *Lettre*, 29. This paragraph and the two preceding it are substantially and in part verbally identical with two paragraphs from §8.

§13[1]

≈

(119) We have been delivered from the necessity of that slavery by the one who gives us not only the law's precepts, but also love by way of the Spirit, so that delight in sin might be vanquished by delight in love. Otherwise, delight in sin remains always victorious, and always tempts those it holds as slaves. For we are captive to and enslaved by what has vanquished us.[2]

(112) Free choice is unable to do anything but sin if it does not know the way of truth. And even when what it should do begins to be shown to it, it does not do it, does not undertake it, and does not enter upon the good way if that way is not delightful to and loved by it. Love is sown in the heart, not by free choice which comes from us, but by the Holy Spirit, so that our free choice might love the way of truth.[3]

(112) That is why each of us sometimes knows and sometimes does not know to undertake, continue, and accomplish good work; and that sometimes we take delight in it and sometimes not—so that we understand that it is not by our power but by God's gift that we know the good and take delight, and that God gives delight, and the earth that we are returns its fruit.[4]

1. I translate §13 from Le Guern, *Oeuvres*, 2:298–303; see also Mesnard, *Oeuvres*, 3:684–92. §13 is a dossier of twenty-three passages, twenty-two of which are from Augustine, and one from Prosper. All parenthetical numbers in §13 are Pascal's indications of pages from Sinnich. Le Guern divides two of these excerpts into more than one paragraph; I give each as a single paragraph but mark Le Guern's paragraph divisions with ¶.

2. Augustine, *Contra Julianum opus imperfectum* 1.109 (also in §5), from Sinnich, 119.

3. Augustine, *De spiritu* 3.5, from Sinnich, 112.

4. Augustine, *De peccatorum meritis* 2.17.27 (also in §5), from Sinnich, 112–13; Augustine echoes Psalm 85:13.

(113) When we ask him for help to accomplish righteousness, do we ask him for anything other than that he uncover for us what was hidden, and render sweet what does not delight us? And now, by a righteous punishment, vice has come to us, which makes it repugnant to obey righteousness; if that vice is not overcome by the help of grace, no one is turned toward righteousness; and if not healed by the work of grace, no one enjoys the peace of righteousness. We are therefore vanquished and healed by the grace which comes from the one to whom we say, "Turn us!" When he does, it is an act of mercy; when he does not, it is one of righteousness. ⁊And it is for that reason that he waits to heal the saints and the faithful of some vices, so that the good delights them less and does not entirely suffice to accomplish righteousness. In doing this, God wills us not to be damnable, but to be humble.[5]

(269) When the vices habitually vanquish us, we are able to overcome them only with much effort, and that happens truly and sincerely only by way of true delight in righteousness. Therefore, the vices should be judged vanquished when they are vanquished by God's love, which only God gives.[6]

(440) When we take delight in the things that lead to God, that delight is breathed into us and given to us by God's grace, not by our efforts or merits.[7]

(413) Does the mind ever embrace anything without delighting in it? Is it within our power to make the things that delight us come to us, or the things that come to us delight us?[8]

(227) When we begin to be animated by the spirit of God, we incline against the flesh by way of the much more powerful force of love; there may yet remain in us something that resists us, infirmities as yet unhealed; but we are nevertheless righteous and live by faith to the extent that we do not give in to the evil concupiscence which has been vanquished by love of righteousness.[9]

5. Augustine, *De peccatorum meritis* 2.19.33 (also in §§6, 9), from Sinnich, 113.

6. Augustine, *De civitate Dei* 21.16, from Sinnich, 269.

7. Augustine, *Ad Simplicianum* 1.2.21, from Sinnich, 440.

8. Augustine, *Ad Simplicianum* 1.2.21, from Sinnich, 413.

9. Augustine, *Enchiridion* 31.118, from Sinnich, 227.

(414) Although the good begins to be desired when it begins to delight, when we do what is good out of fear of suffering rather than for love of righteousness, we do not yet do good; and we do not do in our hearts the good that seems to be done in our actions so long as we have greater love for not doing it, if we could do so with impunity. Therefore, God's grace is the delight which effects in us delight and desire for what God commands.[10]

(420) As for me, I say to you, "it is not much to say that you should be drawn by the will—you are drawn by pleasure." What is it to be drawn by pleasure? "Find, O soul, your sweetness in the Lord, and he will grant you what your heart asks." There is a pleasure of the heart by which heavenly bread is sweet. For if the poets have been able to say that everyone is drawn by pleasure—not by necessity, but by pleasure; not by constraint, but by delight—how much more reason should we have to say that we are drawn toward Jesus Christ when we are delighted by the truth, by beatitude, by righteousness, and by eternal life! All these are Jesus Christ. Ah, is it possible that the corporeal senses have their pleasures, and the mind be deprived of its? And if the mind lacks its pleasures, how is it written, "the children of men will be drunk with the abundance of your house, and you will satisfy them with the flood of your delights"? Give me one person who loves, and she will know what I speak of; give me one who desires intensely, one who hungers and thirsts and pants for the fountains of the celestial country, and he will know what I speak of; but if I address cold souls, they will not understand me. ❡Show greenery to a sheep and you draw it to yourself; present a nut to babies and they are drawn by love, that is, drawn without violence done to the body, drawn by the bonds of the heart. And so, if things that belong to the goods and pleasures of the earth draw those who love them when they are offered because it is true that "all are driven by what gives them pleasure," will Jesus Christ, revealed by the Father, not have the strength to draw them? For what does the soul desire more strongly than truth?[11]

10. Augustine, *Contra duas epistulas* 2.9.21, from Sinnich, 414.

11. Augustine, *In Johannis evangelium* 26.4, from Sinnich, 420; Augustine echoes Psalm 37:4, Psalm 36:9, and Virgil, *Eclogues* 2.65.

(662) We are reduced to servitude by what vanquishes us. The freedom of slaves subjected to sin can therefore only be in the delight they have in sinning. For those who wholeheartedly do what they want freely follow their masters. In this way, slaves to sin are free to sin. It follows from this that we will never be free to act justly until, delivered from sin, we begin to be slaves to righteousness. That is true freedom, caused by joy in doing what is good; at the same time it is holy servitude, caused by obedience to the precepts. But where does that freedom to do good come from for those enslaved and sold if the one who says "if the Son delivers you, you will be truly free" does not deliver them?[12]

(663) Therefore, free choice is truly free when it is no longer the slave of vice and sin.[13]

(102) We must combat lack; but we will certainly be vanquished if not helped by God in such a way that not only do we see what we must do, but that when health has come to us, delight in righteousness vanquishes and overcomes in us delight in things, desire to possess which or fear of losing which makes us sin accordingly.[14]

(181) Perfect righteousness is clearly unexampled among us, and is nevertheless not impossible—for it would come if we willed it as strongly as necessary, and we would will it in that way if it happened that nothing that belongs to righteousness were unknown to us, and that it delighted our minds in such a way that delight overcame all the pleasure or pain that obstructs it. That does not happen, not because it is impossible, but because of God's judgment. For who does not know that it is not in our power to know something and to have it follow from understanding that we should desire it that we do desire it, unless we take as much delight in it as we should have love for it?[15]

(145) The will which is free with respect to evil because it finds its delight there is not free with respect to good because it has not been handed over to it.[16]

12. Augustine, *Enchiridion* 9.30, from Sinnich, 662; Augustine quotes John 8:36.
13. Augustine, *De civitate Dei* 14.11, from Sinnich, 663.
14. Augustine, *Enchiridion* 22.81 (also in §5), from Sinnich, 102.
15. Augustine, *De spiritu* 35.63, from Sinnich, 181.
16. Augustine, *Contra duas epistulas* 1.3.6, from Sinnich, 145.

(148) Therefore, "power is given so that those who believe in God might become God's children"—that very power is given so that they might believe in God; such ability cannot belong to free choice unless given by God, because choice will not be free with respect to good unless the Redeemer has delivered it there; but it is free with respect to evil, either because delight in evil has been infused by the enemy, whether hidden or manifest, or because it has procured it for itself.[17]

(209) That empty and consequently evil greediness vanquishes and brings to a halt other evil greedinesses, and they are called continent because of that.[18]

(394) When one delight dies, another yet lives; those who do not consent to a living desire move it toward death. When we begin no longer to be delighted by a desire, we move it toward death. That is our business, our battle. In that combat, God is our spectator when we fight; when we tire, we turn to his help; for if he does not help us, we are unable not only to win, but even to fight.[19]

(253) Those who do not sin out of fear of pain are enemies to righteousness; they become its friends when it is out of love that they do not sin. For those who fear torture do not fear sin—they are frightened to burn ... for all who hate sin as much as they love righteousness are able to do so only by grace.[20]

(366) God makes it so we will what we did not will, variously redirecting the infidelity of those who resist him so that, engendering and placing in us delight in obeying him, the hearts of those who listen lift themselves above what was weighing them down, learn what they were ignorant of, and trust what they mistrusted. For "the Lord gives delight, and the earth we are returns fruit."[21]

17. Augustine, *Contra duas epistulas* 1.3.7, from Sinnich, 148; Augustine quotes John 1:12.

18. Augustine, *Contra Julianum* 4.3.18, from Sinnich, 209.

19. Augustine, *Sermones* 156.9.9, from Sinnich, 394.

20. Augustine, *Epistulae* 145.4, from Sinnich, 253; the ellipses follow Le Guern, *Oeuvres*, 2:302 and indicate Pascal's omission of some sentences from the excerpt Sinnich provides.

21. Prosper, *De gratia Dei* 6, from Sinnich, 366; Prosper quotes Psalm 85:13.

(466) We pray in the Psalm, "Lord, you are sweet; sweetly teach us your righteousness," so that we might not be bound under the law in a servile way by fear of pain, but by free love might find ourselves delighted to be with your law; for it is such delight which freely accomplishes the law, making it so that it is done voluntarily—those who learn in this way, do everything they have learned.[22]

(467) The letter itself kills—it makes transgressors when it commands the good and does not give the love which alone wills the good.[23]

(270) Since we can be without sin in this life when grace helps our wills, why does this not happen? I can reply very easily and truly that it is because we do not will it. But if you ask me why we do not, a long discussion ensues. Nonetheless, without prejudice to a more precise investigation, I can say briefly that we do not will what is righteous either because what is righteous does not seem so to us, or because it does not delight us. That is because we will something with an ardor as great as the certainty with which we understand it to be good coupled with the power of the delight we take in it. And so, ignorance and weakness are the vices that obstruct the will, whether to do good or cease to do evil. It is therefore necessary that divine grace help our wills, whether by instructing us about what we are ignorant of, or by making it so that we find sweet what does not delight us.[24]

22. Augustine, *De gratia Christi* 1.13.14, from Sinnich, 466.
23. Augustine, *Contra Julianum opus imperfectum* 1.94, from Sinnich, 467.
24. Augustine, *De peccatorum meritis* 2.17.26, from Sinnich, 270.

§14[1]

≈

Conc. Valent., 3—<impossible, that's to say to love | ch. | forces are lacking | For.>—Verum aliquos ad malum praedestinatos esse divina potestate, videlicet ut quasi aliud esse non possint, non solum non credimus, sed etiam si sint qui tantum mali credere velint, cum omni detestatione sicut Arausica synodus: Illis anathema dicimus.[2]

1. I translate §14 from Le Guern, *Oeuvres*, 2:303–8; see also Mesnard, *Oeuvres*, 3:737–45. §14 consists almost entirely of twenty-seven brief excerpts from patristic and conciliar texts in Latin. Le Guern's edition divides the longer of these excerpts into paragraphs; I indicate those divisions by a paragraph mark (¶), but otherwise render them as a single block of text. At the beginning of each excerpt, Pascal provides an abbreviated reference to the original source, which is in most cases not the immediate source he took it from; and, for most of the excerpts, he also provides some compressed, probably mnemonic, marginal comments, some in very abbreviated form, and some as brief phrases in French. I place these marginal comments within angle brackets (<...>) in what seems the appropriate place within each excerpt, leaving the briefest of them in the form they appear in Le Guern's edition, and translating the longer ones from French into English. The marginal comments are divided from one another by a vertical line (|). A note to each excerpt provides, first, an English rendering of it; then a reference in up-to-date form; then the source from which Pascal took the excerpt. I give an English rendering even when Pascal translates some or all of an excerpt elsewhere in the *Writings*, because he often translates freely, and it seems good to give anglophone readers a closer rendering of the dossier of excerpts in §14 than Pascal does.

2. "Not only do we not believe that some are predestined to evil by divine power as if they could not be otherwise, but even if there might be any who would want to believe such an evil thing, then, in accord with the Council of Orange, we anathematize them with complete abhorrence."—Pascal's immediate source for this excerpt from the canons of the Third Council of Valence is unclear, though see Arnauld, *Seconde lettre*, 122–23.

Conc. Arausic. 2, c. 25—<why are they possible? | why or how?>—
Aliquos vero ad malum divina potestate praedestinatos esse non solum
non credimus, sed etiam si sunt qui tantum malum credere velint, cum
omni detestatione: Illis anathema dicimus.[3]

Aug., De perf. just., *c. 10*—<Char. | impossible, that's to say | How?>—
Deinde iste adhibet testimonia quibus ostendat non esse gravia divina
praecepta. Quis autem nesciat, cum praeceptum sit generale charitas,
et plenitudo legis est charitas, non esse grave quod *diligendo fit,* non
timendo?[4] Laborant autem in Dei praeceptis qui ea timendo conantur
implere, sed perfecta charitas foras mittit timorem et facit praecepti
sarcinam non solum non praementem onere ponderum, verum etiam
sublevantem vice pennarum, etc. ¶<ch. | Forces are lacking | why? | For.
| How?> Nec aliam ob causam Scriptura commemorat non esse gravia
divina praecepta, nisi ut anima quae illa gravia sentit intelligat se nondum *accepisse vires* quibus talia sint praecepta Domini qualia commen-
dantur levia scilicet atque suavia, et orat gemitu voluntatis ut impetret
donum facultatis, etc. ¶<Char. | How? | For. | Why?> Commendantur
ergo non esse gravia, ut cui gravia sunt intelligat nondum se accepisse
donum quo gravia non sint, nec arbitretur ea se perficere quando ita
facit ut gravia sint, hilarem enim datorem diligit Dominus. ¶<Ch > Et
mandata ejus gravia non sunt, debent utique commoneri charitati Dei
non esse grave mandatum.[5]

3. "Not only do we not believe that some are predestined to evil by divine power,
but even if there are any who would want to believe such an evil thing, we anathematize
them with complete abhorrence."—Pascal's immediate source for this excerpt from
the canons of the Second Council of Orange may be Arnauld, *Seconde lettre,* 122–23.

4. Le Guern, *Oeuvres,* 2:304, lacks this question mark, which sense strongly suggests. Mesnard, *Oeuvres,* 3:738, has it.

5. "In what follows are testimonies that show the divine precepts not to be burdensome. Who does not know that, since the general precept is one of love, and love
the accomplishment of the law, that *what is done by love,* rather than fear, is not burdensome? Those who want to accomplish God's precepts out of fear have to work at
it, but perfect love casts out fear and makes the burden of the precepts not only not
a crushing weight, but one that lifts it up as with wings, and so on. ¶Scripture notes
that the divine precepts are not burdensome for no other reason than that the soul,
experiencing them in that way, should understand itself not yet *to have accepted the
powers* by which the Lord's precepts become as they are commended, which is to say

Prosp., Ep. ad Demetr.—Nec ob aliud unquam datur praeceptum, nisi ut quaeratur praecipientis auxilium.[6]

Aug., De pecc. et merit. et remiss., *c. 3*—<Object.>—Acute sibi videntur dicere quasi nostrum hoc ullus ignoret *quod si nolumus non peccamus, nec praeciperet Deus quod esset humanae impossibile voluntati.*[7]

Aug., De pecc. merit., *c. 6.*—<How?>—Nam qui dicunt esse posse in hac vita hominem sine peccato, non est eis continuo incauta temeritate obsistendum. Si enim esse posse negaverimus, et hominis libero arbitrio qui hoc volendo appetit, et Dei virtuti vel misericordiae qui hoc adjuvando efficit, derogabimus.[8]

Aug., De natura et grat., *c. 42 et 43.*—<Passage of the Council: habit. and act>—Neque de ipsa possibilitate contendo cum *sanata* et *adjuta*

---

light and gentle; and should pray with groans of the will to obtain the gift of the capacity, and so on. ¶The precepts are commended, therefore, as not burdensome, so that those for whom they are so might understand themselves not yet to have accepted the gift that makes them not so, and should not judge themselves to be perfecting them when undertaking them as if they were burdensome, for the Lord loves those who give with joy. Also, his commandments are not burdensome, for to share in God's love is no heavy burden."—Augustine, *De perfectione* 10.21 (also in §§1, 10), probably from Augustine, *Opera*, 7:511–12.

6. "The precepts are not given for any other reason than that those commanded might look for help."—Prosper, *Epistula ad Demetriadem* 15 (also in §10), from Sinnich, 179.

7. "They think themselves acute in saying, as if we did not know it, that since *there is no sin without will, God would not have commanded what is impossible for us to will.*"—Augustine, *De peccatorum meritis* 2.3.3 (also in §2), perhaps from Augustine, *Opera*, 7:292. There are difficulties with the Latin here. Le Guern, *Oeuvres*, 2:304, reads: Acute sibi videntur dicere quasi nostrum hoc ullus ignoret *quod si nolumus non peccamus, nec praeciperet Deus quod si nolumus non peccamus, nec praeciperet Deus quod esset humanae impossibile voluntati*, which dittographs *quod si nolumus non peccamus, nec praeciperet Deus*. See Mesnard, *Oeuvres*, 3:739, which reads *voluntatis* for *voluntati*, which makes less good sense and is the reading neither in the edition cited nor in Sinnich, which Pascal had also consulted, as is evident in §2.

8. "It is not necessary to oppose continuously with incautious rashness those who say that it is possible for us to be without sin in this life. For if we were to deny this to be possible, we would detract from both our free choice, which is eager for it, and God's power or mercy, which makes it happen by helping."—Augustine, *De peccatorum meritis* 2.6.7, probably from Augustine, *Opera*, 7:293.

hominis voluntate possibilitas ipsa simul cum effectu in sanctis proveniat, dum charitas Dei, etc. diffunditur, etc. ¶And two or three lines later: Who doesn't know that God created us holy? Sed nunc de illo agitur quem semivivum latrones reliquerunt, etc. ¶Non igitur Deus impossibilia jubet, sed jubendo admonet et facere quod possis et petere quod non possis. Jam nunc videamus unde possit. Iste (Pelagius) dicet: *Voluntatis non est quod natura potest.* Ego dico voluntatis quidem non est homo justus, nec natura potest, sed medicina poterit quod vitio non potest.[9]

Aug., De nat. et grat., *c. 69.*—<How? | Ch. | affect. act. | Why?>—Eo quippe ipso quo firmissime creditur Deum justum et bonum impossibilia non potuisse praecipere, hinc admonemur et in facilibus quid agamus, et in difficilibus quid petamus. Omne quippe facilia sunt charitati cui uni Christi sarcina levis est, aut ea una est sarcina ipsa quae levis est. Secundum hoc dictum est, praecepta ejus gravia non sunt, ut cui gravia sunt consideret non potuisse dici gravia non sunt nisi quia[10] potest esse cordis affectus cui gravia non sint, etc. Aut enim quisque non diligit, ed ideo grave est, aut diligit, et grave esse non potest, etc. Utrumque verum est, durae sunt timori, leves charitati.[11]

---

9. "Without arguing for the possibility that, when someone's will has been *healed* and *helped*, that possibility occurs for those saints at the same time as its effect, so long as God's love, etc., is spread abroad, etc. ¶ … they are now half dead like those the robbers abandoned, etc. ¶It is not therefore that God commands what is impossible, but by commanding, he indicates that we should do what we can and ask for what we cannot. Now let us see whence this ability comes. That one (Pelagius) will say: *what nature can do does not belong to the will.* I say that none are righteous by will, and neither is nature able; but by healing, the will becomes able to do what lack cannot."—Augustine, *De natura* 42.49–43.50 (also in §1), from Sinnich, 157–58. The underlined words are from Romans 5:5, and there is a clear echo of Luke 10:25–37.

10. Le Guern, *Oeuvres*, 2:305, reads *qui* for *quia* here. *Quia*, however, makes better sense; it is what Augustine, *Opera*, 7:324 reads (the edition Pascal was probably using here); it is given by Mesnard, *Oeuvres*, 3:740; and it is the reading of most modern editions of *De natura*.

11. "The very same thing by which it is to be most firmly believed that a righteous and good God is unable to command what is impossible indicates to us that we should do what is easy and ask for help with what is difficult. For everything is easy for love, for which alone Christ's burden is light—or, love is itself the light burden. Accordingly, it is said that his commands are not burdensome so that those for whom they are

Aug, l. 1 Oper. imperf., *n. 7.*—<Resp.>—Non est mirum quod novi haeretici catholicis a quibus exeunt novum nomen imponunt; hoc et alii fecerunt quando similiter exierunt.[12]

123. Julian. Aug., l. 2 Operis imperf., *n. 76.*—<Obj.>—Et qui expavissent ne a vobis Pelagiani dicerentur, in Manichaeorum pelagus praecipitarentur, etc. Ne igitur vocentur haeretici, fiunt Manichaei, et dum falsam verentur infamiam, verum crimen incurrunt.[13]

Aug., l. 2 De nupt. et conc., *c. 3.*—<Resp.>—Non est ita. Multum falleris vel fallere meditaris, non liberum negamus arbitrium.[14]

Julian 132. Aug.., l. ad Bonif., *c. 2.*—<Obj.>—Dicunt, inquit, illi Manichaei quibus modo non communicamus, id est toti illi quibus dissentimus, quia primi hominis peccato, id est Adae, liberum arbitrium perierit, et nemo jam potestatem habeat bene vivendi, sed omnes in peccatum carnis suae necessitate cogi.[15]

Valentinus. 132. Ibid., *c. 15.*—<object.>—Contra haec, inquit, nos cotidie disputamus et ideo nolumus praevaricatoribus adhibere consensum,

---

burdensome should consider that it could not be said that they are not burdensome were it not that it is possible to have a disposition of the heart for which they are not, etc. For those who do not love, they are burdensome, and for those who do, they cannot be, etc. Both are true: they are hard for those who fear, and light for those who love."—Augustine, *De natura* 69.83 (also in §§1, 9, 10, 15), probably from Augustine, *Opera,* 7:324.

12. "It is no surprise that new heretics impose a new name upon the Catholics they have left; others did so when they left."—Augustine, *Contra Julianum opus imperfectum* 1.6 (also in §2), from Sinnich, 125.

13. "Those who fear being called Pelagians by you fall into the ocean of the Manichaeans, etc. To avoid being called heretics, they become Manicheans; avoiding a false insult, they fall into a real offense."—Augustine, *Contra Julianum opus imperfectum* 1.75 (also in §2), quoting Julian; from Sinnich, 123; Pascal following Sinnich, mislocates this excerpt in the second book of the *Contra Julianum.*

14. "This is not so. You are much deceived, or you are trying to deceive others. We do not deny free choice."—Augustine, *De nuptiis* 2.3.8 (also in §2), from Sinnich, 124.

15. "<Julian> said that the Manichees, with whom we have no communication, say that because of the sin of Adam, the first human, free choice perished, and no one is now able to live well, while all are compelled to sin by the necessity of the flesh—and from that we dissent completely."—Augustine, *Contra duas epistulas* 1.2.4, from Sinnich, 132.

quia nos dicimus liberum arbitrium in omnibus esse naturaliter, nec Adae peccato perire potuisse, quod Scripturarum omnium autoritate firmatur.[16]

132. Pelagius in Epist. ad pap. *Innoc. Aug., Lib. de grat. Chr., c. 31.*—<Obj.>—Quam liberi arbitrii potestatem dicimus in omnibus esse generaliter, in Christianis, Judaeis, atque gentilibus; in omnibus est liberum arbitrium aequaliter per naturam, sed in solis Christianis adversus peccatum a gratia.[17]

133. Julianus. Aug., l. 1 Oper. imp., n. 98.—<Obj.>—Hoc ergo liberum arbitrium, etc. sicut catholici omnes confitentur: ita vos non solum cum Manichaeo sed etiam cum Joviniano quem nobis audes impingere,[18] diverso quidem genere, sed impietate simili denegatis.[19]

L. 1 ad Bonif., c. 2.—<Resp.>—Quis autem nostrum dicat quod primi hominis peccato perierit liberum arbitrium? De humano quidem genere libertas periit per peccatum, sed illa quae in paradiso fuit.[20]

---

16. "It is against this, he <Julian> said, that we dispute every day; we do not wish to hold to the consensus of the transgressors, and so we assert that free choice is naturally in all and was not able to perish because of Adam's sin—which is confirmed by the authority of the entirety of Scripture."—Augustine, *Contra duas epistulas* 1.15.29 (also in §2), from Sinnich, 132; the attribution to Valentinus is not in Sinnich, and may be Pascal's contribution, perhaps in reference to the Abbot of Hadrumetum, who bore this name and to whom Augustine's *De gratia et libero arbitrio* is dedicated. The opinion quoted, however, is Julian's.

17. "We <Pelagians> hold that this power of free choice is in all of us generally, in Christians, Jews, and gentiles. It is equally in all by nature, but only in Christians is it directed against sin by grace."—Augustine, *De gratia Christi* 1.31.33 (also in §2), quoting Pelagius; from Sinnich, 132.

18. Le Guern, *Oeuvres*, 2:306, reads *impigere* for *impingere*. But *impingere* makes better sense; it is the reading at Sinnich, 133, and at Mesnard, *Oeuvres*, 3:742. It is also the reading of modern editions of the *Contra Julianum opus imperfectum*.

19. "This free choice, etc., which all Catholics acknowledge: you [Augustine] deny it, differently but with similar ungodliness, not only with Mani but also with Jovinian—whom you dare to attach to us <Pelagians>."—Augustine, *Contra Julianum opus imperfectum* 1.96 (also in §2), from Sinnich, 133.

20. "Who among us <Catholics> says that free choice perished because of the first human's sin? Certainly, freedom of a kind perished from humankind by sin, but that was the freedom of paradise."—Augustine, *Contra duas epistulas* 1.2.5 (also in §2),

Prosp. ad Ruff.—<Resp.>—Nimium vero inepte nimiumque inconsiderate ab adversantibus dicitur quod per hanc Dei gratiam libero nihil relinquitur arbitrio.[21]

Prosper, Resp. ad Capit. 6 Gall.—<Obj. | Resp.>—Liberum arbitrium nihil esse vel non esse perperam dicitur, sed ante illuminationem fidei in tenebris illud et in umbra mortis agere non recte negatur.[22]

Prosp., Epist ad Demetr.—<Object. | Resp.>—An forte verendum est ne liberum tollere videamur arbitrium, cum omnia per quae propitiatur Deus ad ipsum dicimus esse referenda?[23]

Aug., Epist, *89, q. 2.*—<Resp.>—Neque enim voluntatis arbitrium ideo tollitur quia juvatur, sed ideo juvatur quia non tollitur.[24]

Aug., De spir. et litt., c. 29.—<Resp.> Liberum ergo arbitrium evacuamus per gratiam? Absit. Sed magis liberum arbitrium statuimus. Sicut enim lex per fidem, sic liberum arbitrium per gratiam non evacuatur, sed statuitur.[25]

153. Aug., l. 1 Oper. imperf., n. 117.—<Man.>—Porro autem Manichaeus nec omnem naturam in quantum natura est dicit bonam, nec eam quam dicit naturam malam ullo modo dicit sanari posse et fieri bonam.[26]

---

from Sinnich, 137; Sinnich misattributes this excerpt to Prosper, an error which Pascal follows neither here nor in §2.

21. "It is excessively foolish and unconsidered of our enemies to say that God's grace leaves nothing to free choice."—Prosper, *Epistula ad Rufinum* 8 (also in §2, but there attributed by Pascal, mistakenly, to Augustine), from Sinnich, 137.

22. "To say that free choice is nothing or is not is to speak wrongly; in the darkness before the illumination of faith, and in the shadow of death, it is not rightly denied."—Prosper, *Responsiones* 6 (also in §2), from Sinnich, 139.

23. "Should we fear that it seems we remove free choice when we say that everything pleasing to God should be referred to him?"—Prosper, *Epistula ad Demetriadem* 13, from Sinnich, 140.

24. "The will's choice is not denied because it is helped; rather, it is helped because it is not denied."—Augustine, *Epistulae* 157.2.10 (also in §2), from Sinnich, 140.

25. "Do we therefore empty out free choice by way of grace? Not at all. Rather, we establish it. Free choice is not emptied out but established by grace, as is the law by faith."—Augustine, *De spiritu* 30.52 (also in §2), from Sinnich, 141.

26. "Further, Mani calls no nature, in so far as it is a nature, good; neither does he say the nature he calls evil can in any way be said to be capable of being healed or of

n. 99.—<Manich.>—Ac per hoc mirabiliter demens naturam mali vult esse immutabilem.[27]

131. Pelag., Libell. fidei ad Innoc. *apud Aug.,* Serm. *191 de tempore.*—<Manich.> Liberum sic confitemur arbitrium ut dicamus nos Dei semper indigere auxilio, et tam illos errare qui cum Manichaeo dicunt hominem peccatum vitare non posse quam illos qui cum Joviniano asserunt hominem non posse peccare. Uterque enim tollit arbitrii libertatem. Nos vero dicimus hominem semper et peccare et non peccare posse, ut nos liberi confiteamur esse arbitrii.[28]

Hyer., Ad Celant.—<The precepts oblige everyone>—Hoc itaque duplex (declina a malo, et fac bonum) diversumque praeceptum, prohibendi scilicet et imperandi, aequo omnibus jure mandatum est; non virgo, non nupta, ab hoc imperio libera est. In quovis proposito, in quovis gradu aequale peccatum est, vel prohibita admittere, vel jussa non facere.[29]

Hyer., Ad Ctesiph.—<Difficulties | None>—Si facilia, [profer qui ea] impleverit, et cur David in Psalmo canat, etc. ¶Si autem difficilia, cur ausus es dicere facilia esse Dei mandata, quae nullus impleverit? ¶Soletis et hoc dicere: aut possibilia sunt Dei mandata et recte a Deo data, aut impossibilia, et non in his esse culpam qui accepere mandata, sed in eo qui dedit impossibilia, etc. ¶<Object.> Possibilia, inquit, mandata dedit Deus. Et quis hoc negat? Sed quomodo intelligenda sit sententia, vas

---

doing good."—Augustine, *Contra Julianum opus imperfectum* 1.115 (also in §2), from Sinnich, 153.

27. "Wonderfully demented, he <Mani> wants the nature of evil to be immutable."—Augustine, *Contra Julianum opus imperfectum* 1.97 (also in §2), from Sinnich, 154.

28. "We acknowledge free choice so that we can say that we are always in need of God's help, and to show the error of those who say with Mani that we are unable to escape sin, as well as those who assert with Jovinian that we are unable to sin. Both remove freedom of choice. We say, rather, that we are always able to sin or not to; in that way we can acknowledge that there is free choice."—Pelagius, *Libellus fidei* 6, from Sinnich, 132; Pascal's reference to the page number of Sinnich is incorrect.

29. "This bidirectional precept, (turn from evil, do good), prohibiting and prescribing, is legally mandated equally for all. Neither virgins nor married women are free from this prescription. Whatever the topic and whatever the level, it is equally sinful to do something prohibited as to fail to do something commanded."—Jerome, *Epistulae* 148.5, perhaps from Jerome, *Epistolae,* 42.

electionis apertissime dicet. <Resp.> Ait enim: *Quod erat impossibile legi*, et *Deus mittens filium suum*, etc. ¶<Object.> Reclamabis, et dices Manichaeorum nos sequi.[30]

Hyer., lib. 1 Adversus Pel.—Aut possibilia Deus mandata dedit, aut impossibilia. Si possibilia, in nostra potestate est ea facere si velimus. Si impossibilia, nec in eo rei sumus si non facimus quod implere non possumus; <Object.> ac per hoc sive possibilia dedit Deus mandata sive impossibilia, potest homo sine peccato esse si volet. ¶<Impossible | Arts> Multas artes possibiles, sed quis omnes simul cum unam vix duas nemo dixerit posse. ¶Vides ergo quod Deus possibilia jusserit, et tamen id quod possibile est per naturam nullum posse complere. ¶<Impossible for us | Power from God> Neque intelligis quae proposueris. Neque enim homo potest esse sine peccato, quod tua habet sententia, sed potest si voluerit Deus hominem servare sine peccato.[31]

30. "If easy, present the one who has accomplished them, and why David sings in the Psalm, etc. ¶If difficult, why do you undertake to call God's commands easy when no one has accomplished them? ¶You are accustomed to saying that either God's commands are possible and rightly given by God, or impossible, in which case there is no fault in those who receive the commands, but rather in the one who gave impossible commands, etc. ¶Pelagius says that the commands God gave are possible. Who denies it? But how can the sentence, he will say that the vessel of election is fully open, be understood? For he said: *What was impossible to the law*, and, *God sending his son*, etc. ¶You will protest and say that we follow the Manichees."—Jerome, *Epistulae* 133.3–4 (also in §2), perhaps from Jerome, *Epistolae*, 266; Pascal's excerpt is discontinuous and compressed; it omits most of Jerome's scriptural examples, the point of which is to show that there is no contradiction between saying that the commandments can be kept, and saying that only God's grace makes them capable of being kept.

31. "Either God has given possible commands, or impossible ones. If possible, we are able to do them should we will to. If impossible, we are not responsible for not doing what it is impossible for us to accomplish. And so, whether God gave possible or impossible commands, we are able to be without sin if we so will ... ¶Many arts are possible, but who will say that they are all possible at once when one can have one with difficulty and no one can have two? ... ¶You can see, then, that God has commanded possible things, and that no one is able naturally to accomplish what is possible. ... ¶You do not understand what you propose <about Jude 1:24, which Jerome's opponent has taken to mean that sinlessness is possible>. We are not able to be without sin, as you like to say; but God is able, should he will it, to preserve us without sin."—Jerome, *Dialogus* 1.21–1.24; perhaps from Jerome, *Epistolae*, 274–75, which Pascal here condenses as much as quotes, to the point of unintelligibility.

§15[1]

[Molinists][2]

…God had an identical, equal, general, and conditional will to save all so long as they willed it, leaving it to their free choice to will it, or not, by means of the sufficient grace he gives to all by the merits of Jesus Christ.

Accordingly, the fact that some are saved and some are not is not a result of God's absolute will, but of our will.

Their error consists in this.

Calvinists[3]

God, in creating us in Adam, had an absolute will, independent of foreknowledge of any merit or demerit, to save some and to damn others. In order to bring about that result, God made Adam sin, together with all of us in him, so that since we are all offenders, he could justly damn those he had resolved to damn in their creation; he sent Jesus Christ for the redemption only of those he had resolved to save in creating them. All this is full of error.

These are the three opinions lively today.[4] That of the Calvinists is so horrible, and assaults the mind so violently with a view of God's

---

1. I translate §15 from Le Guern, *Oeuvres*, 2:308–16; see also Mesnard, *Oeuvres*, 3:766–81.

2. Le Guern, *Oeuvres*, 2:308, supplies this heading, and clearly something is missing at the beginning of §15. I follow him in placing it within brackets.

3. Pascal's principal source for this discussion of the Calvinists is Bourzeis, *Saint Augustin victorieux*, 108–44.

4. Only two have been mentioned in §15; the third would have been the Augustinian view.

cruelty toward his creatures, that it is insupportable. By contrast, that of the Molinists is so gentle and so conformable to common sense that it is entirely charming and agreeable. That of the Church occupies the middle: it is neither as cruel as Calvin's nor as gentle as Molina's. But because we should not judge truth by appearances, we must examine the three views at their root.

To begin this examination, we must fill our minds with the magnitude of original sin and of the wound it gave to humankind.

We must consider how much our condition at our creation differs from our condition after sin.

In Adam, at the hour of our creation, we were righteous, pleasing to God, and submissive.

We are also, in Adam after his transgression, sinners, abominable to God and in revolt against him. Adam's sin, transmitted to all his posterity, is of such enormity that we cannot conceive its magnitude; it is enough to say that it was necessary for God to become incarnate in order to expiate it, and that he suffered to death in order to make evil's magnitude understood by measuring it with the magnitude of its remedy.

It is for this reason that the Church, considering us in these two different conditions, has two very different thoughts about God's will for our salvation and our damnation.

She recognizes in God an equal, general, and conditional will for our salvation at the moment of our creation.

But she also recognizes in God an absolute will unfailingly to save some after sin, and to leave others after the same sin, with no will to save them.

A lack of distinction between these two conditions is the source of the errors of both Calvinists and Molinists. Aspiration for singularity has led these weak ones who have invented these errors on the one hand to think of God's will for offenders as single, and to establish in God an absolute will to damn some and save others at the point of their creation.

And the others, considering God's will for the innocent, have extended it also to offenders, and have established in God a general and conditional will to save all of them.

And so, we and the Molinists are in complete agreement about the thought that God wills our salvation at our creation; but we differ about God's will after Adam's fall.

The Calvinists differ horribly from us about God's will at our creation, while we agree verbally about God's absolute will for redemption; we differ, however, about the sense of those words, in that we understand that God's decree is subsequent to his foreknowledge of Adam's sin, and applied to offenders; they, however, claim that the command is not only prior to but the cause of Adam's fall, and applied to those as yet innocent.

Accordingly, Molinists claim that predestination and reprobation occur by way of foreknowledge of our merits and sins.

Calvinists claim that predestination and reprobation follow God's absolute will. And the Church claims that predestination comes from God's absolute will, and reprobation from foreknowledge of sin.

Accordingly, the Molinists make our will the source of salvation and damnation.

Calvinists do the same for God's will.

The Church makes God's will the source of salvation, and ours the source of damnation.

Now that these opinions have been clarified, it is necessary to show the truth of the Church's and the falsity of the others.

The rule we follow to do that will be the tradition of the Church's doctrine from Jesus Christ to ourselves. We shall show that we find it in our immediate ancestors, they in those that preceded them, they in turn from others, they from the ancient Fathers, who took it from the apostles, who received it directly from Jesus Christ himself, who is the truth.

In this way, we base ourselves upon the unbreakable rock of the gospel and the Holy Scriptures; and we explicate this not following our intellectual proclivities, but those of the ancient Fathers, the popes, the councils, and the prayers of the Church.

That is the rule we follow. It is proper to the Catholic Church, and it excludes the heretics who base themselves upon the truth of Scripture but twist its sense by their idiosyncratic explanations, as they do today on the topic of the reality of Jesus Christ's body in the Eucharist by way of their refusal to acquiesce to the tradition of the Fathers and the councils.

In what follows, we will make clear the novelty of Molina's and Calvin's opinions, which they recognize themselves, so that comparison of the antiquity of the Church's opinion with the novelty of these others provides the view one ought to have of each, and that respect for this crowd of holy defenders of the Church … in the spirit of the faithful the belief … who were one in their views when they arrived at them.[5]

And although it is not necessary to put forward other proofs of the truth, and of the falsity of these other opinions, we will not leave aside response to those passages of Scripture which one or other of these strays explicate following the sense they give to them, and which seem to favor them.

And although common sense need not concur with a matter of faith, we will not leave aside responding to objections from one or other of these. And finally, we will show the extent to which this doctrine itself conforms to common sense.

The principal question in play is whether God has a general will to save all, or whether there are any he does not will to save. Or, what is the same, whether God gives graces sufficient for their salvation to all, or whether there are some to whom he refuses them. Or, what is the same, whether predestination is a result of God's absolute will, which wills to save some but not all.

This is why it is necessary to show in what follows the tradition that all the doctors have always established as a constant truth: that God does not will to save all; that God does not give to all graces sufficient for their salvation; and that predestination is without foreknowledge of works.

First, we have a large number of learned and illustrious defenders of St. Augustine's doctrine, among whom this century has been honored by a particular gift of God to his Church,[6] and who today defend this proposition against the Molinists who wish to abolish it.

---

5. The ellipses in this paragraph follow Le Guern, *Oeuvres*, 2:311, in indicating lacunae. There are various proposals for completing the text. See Le Guern, *Oeuvres*, 2:1247.

6. Perhaps the *don particulier de Dieu* is Jansenius, or possibly Arnauld, or possibly all the Port-Royalists.

These people were preceded by a large number of others, among whom one of the most prominent is Florent Conrius, Archbishop of Ireland, who has defended it and unpacked it at length in his book published not long since, called *Peregrinus Hiericontinus*.[7]

At about the same time, the entire order of Prémontré resolved at a provincial chapter approved by its general:

*that on the topic of grace, all should follow the views of St. Augustine—*which is without doubt just what it seems.[8] A little later, the two celebrated faculties of Louvain and Douai censured the new opinions of the Molinists, which the Jesuits in their time had upheld.[9]

Here is one of the censured propositions:

Since the first, and original, sin, God has had the will to give Adam and all his posterity means sufficient against sin and help to acquire eternal life. The Douai faculty censured this in these terms:

The terms of this assertion are repugnant to the Holy Scriptures, and to the Fathers; they also appear to destroy the proper and true grace of Jesus Christ which, following St. Augustine, is not shared by the good and the wicked, but distinguishes them.

And then it adds: *Jesus Christ did not pray for all, and not all were given to him by the Father, for it is said: "I do not pray for the world, but for those you have given me." Therefore, not all have help from God sufficient to acquire their salvation, for otherwise they would be able to acquire it without Jesus Christ praying for them, and without the Father having given them to Jesus Christ, which no Catholic is able to say.*

These learned theologians therefore hold that God does not give to

7. Florent Conrius (1560–1629) was a Franciscan, and Archbishop of Tuam in Ireland. The book mentioned was published in Paris in 1641. Pascal probably depends here on Arnauld, *Jansénius*, 342.

8. Pascal follows here Arnauld, *Jansénius*, 341.

9. These censures occurred in 1621. Pascal seems here dependent upon the account and the texts given in Arnauld, *Jansénius*, 332–40, and possibly also that in Arnauld, *Saints Pères*, 352–59. Arnauld, in turn, depends upon the *Censurae*, 83–124, and all the quotations in the next twenty or so paragraphs come from there, mediated to Pascal via Arnauld, *Jansénius*, 333–36. Arnauld quotes selectively in Latin from the pages noted, and translates what he selects into French; Pascal selects further from Arnauld, sometimes condensing what he selects, and following exactly neither Arnauld's French nor his Latin.

all helps sufficient to acquire salvation; therefore, according to them, God does not will to save all exactly because he does not give them what they would need for it—and that is what we wanted to show.

Another proposition of the Jesuits from that time: *All Scripture is full of precepts and exhortations aimed at the conversion of sinners to God; but God does not command impossible things; therefore, he gives them help sufficient to make them able to convert.*

Here is how these very learned theologians censured that proposition: *That conclusion is ridiculous; for that very one who commands us to act commands us also to ask for what we are unable to do, which is to say what we have no means sufficient to accomplish; that is why St. Augustine says, "God commands things impossible for us so that we might recognize what we must ask him for." If some of those who ask are unable to do what they ask for, many fewer of those who do not ask will be able to; fewer still among those who do not want to ask God; and yet fewer among those who do not even recognize what it is they should ask of him.*

If it is true that sufficient help is present to all even before it is asked for, it would be necessary to reject the greater part of the Lord's Prayer and the prayers of the Church, for as St. Augustine says, "What is more ridiculous than to ask—to pray—to accomplish what is within our power?"[10]

It appears in this censure how many of the great doctors ...[11] that God does not give his graces to all, and therefore, that God does not will to save all without exception; we therefore cannot be saved without grace.

Here is another proposition from the same Jesuits: *God willed to give Jesus Christ for the redemption of all, without the exception even of one; therefore, he willed to give sufficient help to all by Jesus Christ; for Jesus Christ is redeemer of all only to the extent that he gives them sufficient help to relieve them of their sins, for if sufficient help were not given*

10. Neither Arnauld nor Pascal identifies the quotations from Augustine the Douai faculty use; the first of them, in the preceding paragraph, is from *De natura* 69.83 (also in §§1, 9, 10, 14); the second, in this paragraph, is from *De natura* 18.20. Le Guern, *Oeuvres*, 2:313, separates *before being asked for* from *it would be necessary to reject*, and marks a lacuna in the manuscript. But the sentence makes good sense as written, and so I (re)join the phrases.

11. The ellipses indicate that something is missing here; Le Guern, *Oeuvres*, 2:313, marks a space in the principal manuscript.

them, he would not be their true redeemer because he would be for them neither sufficient nor effective.

And here is the censure of that illustrious faculty:

The sufficiency demanded by the general redemption brought about by Jesus Christ consists in the price of his blood, but not in help given to all, as this proposition claims; were it otherwise, it would be necessary to say that infants unable to be supported by baptism get that help, or at least it would be necessary to say that Jesus Christ did not give himself to them for redemption, and therefore that he did not give himself to all.

It is very evident from this proposition that Jesus Christ did not give himself for the redemption of all; following these theologians, God does not will that all should be saved.

Another proposition of these same Molinist Jesuits: *The burdened and the blind have help sufficient from God for conversion.* And then, below: *All the unfaithful, always and in every connection, have sufficient help from God.*

These are maxims from those who claim that God wills to save all; here are the censures given by the same faculty:

This proposition should be rejected in its entirety as greatly injurious to the good done by Jesus Christ's singular grace, which is not given to all and which is nonetheless necessary for the conversion and salvation of all.

It appears, then, following these theologians, that since the grace of Jesus Christ necessary for salvation is not given to all, God does not will to save those to whom he refuses it.

All the censures confirmed by this same faculty were sent to the Pope in 1591, accompanied by rumor that it had changed its mind; finally, in 1613, that faculty confirmed its renewed censure by the unanimous opinion of all the doctors, and in that act declared:

Although the report has spread in Italy, Spain, and elsewhere, that the Louvain faculty has changed its opinion in the matter of grace, that it has retracted its older censure earlier sent to the Pope, and that it has been brought to do so by the force of Lessius's arguments,[12] *delivered orally and*

---

12. Leonhard Lessius, or Léonard Leys (1554–1623), was a Jesuit theologian with Molinist leanings who taught philosophy at Louvain and Douai, and was a student of Suarez. The censures by the Louvain faculty that Pascal, via Arnauld, discusses, had largely to do with his work.

in print; the Faculty, wanting to oppose the spread of this false report and to make the truth known to all who might wish to know it assembled after the sermon in the small chapter-house of St. Peter's after vespers on 13 July 1613; with none of the doctors disagreeing, the entire faculty declared and attested uniformly that it had held at all times in the past, and continues to hold even in the present, that it has always persisted and continues to persist even in the present in its previous opinions, held and declared in that above-mentioned censure, and that with God's help, it will never distance itself from them. That is, unless it should be otherwise decided, and it should be ordered to believe otherwise by the Pope and the Holy Roman Church, to whose censure and correction it humbly submits all that is contained in the above-mentioned censure, as well as everything it has said elsewhere in addition to everything it might say in the future. The Faculty declares furthermore that rather than Lessius's arguments having caused it to withdraw from its opinions, that as it has at other times improved many things it has said, so now it improves its books and what it has had printed on this matter. The Faculty permits and desires that a copy of this be given to any who ask for it, and that it should be sent everywhere.[13]

It appears very clear that the faculties of Louvain and Douai are of the opinion that God does not give his graces to all, and that this is the same as to say that he does not will all to be saved.

See what the Faculty of Paris says about this at the end of the Master of the Sentences in the Library of the Fathers—these two propositions are condemned:

That God has predestined some from eternity because of some good works they would do.

And:

That God has not predestined so gratuitously those he has predestined that he has not considered either the good works they would do, or those of another.[14]

---

13. Arnauld, *Jansénius*, 339–40.

14. Arnauld, *Jansénius*, 313–15. The propositions Pascal mentions, along with many others, were censured by the Faculty of Paris in 1347. Pascal's location of them *au bout de Maître des sentences* and *dans la Bibliothèque des Pères*, follows Arnauld. Neither identifies editions, but it is probable that the Bibliothèque des Pères indicates the list

It appears, therefore, that at that time, the Faculty of Paris held predestination before foreknowledge of merits, and therefore, because predestination did not come from our wills, it did come from the simple will of God.

St. Thomas, 1a p., q. 23, a. 5, ad 3: *That God chose some and rejected others without our being able to find any cause for the distinction other than his will alone.*

2a2ae, q. 2, a. 5, ad 1: *That God, in punishing actual or original sin, refuses, out of his righteousness, the graces without which we are unable to do the things we are obliged to do, for example, to love God and to believe the articles of faith.*

1a 2ae, q. 106, a. 3, in c.: *That the new law, which is the law of grace, was given only much later, so that we were abandoned to ourselves under the old law, and, falling by ourselves, would recognize our need for grace.*

That all merit to be deprived of grace in punishment for the first sin, and that God therefore acts justly when he does not give it, and mercifully when he does.

Ibid., a. 3: *That God provides sufficiently for us as regards the corporeal life because our nature has not been destroyed by sin; but he does not act in the same way as regards the life of grace and the spiritual life because grace has been destroyed by sin.*

3a p., q. 22, a. 4, ad 2: *Jesus Christ made no unanswered prayer, and so he did not pray to his Father to give life eternal to all those who crucified him, nor to all those who believed in him, but only to the predestined.*[15]

Therefore, following St. Thomas, the opinion that sufficient grace is not given to all is not heretical, but, rather, very Catholic—contra the Molinists.

But this will of God not to save some takes its strength from and has its origins in original sin—contra the Calvinists.

Peter Lombard. See what Peter Lombard, Bishop of Paris and Master of the Sentences, thought:

---

of propositions condemned at Paris in 1347 provided in de La Bigne, 4:1147–1148. It is unclear which edition of the *Sentences* Arnauld refers to.

15. Pascal takes this string of quotations from Thomas's *Summa Theologiae* from Arnauld, *Jansénius*, 308–9, where they are provided in exactly this order. Ferreyrolles provides useful discussion of the significance of these references.

Lib. sent., dist. 41, 46: *He rejects as a very false opinion the view of those who say that God wills that all are to be saved, without a single exception; and he does not recognize that God had that will toward others than those who are actually saved.*
And elsewhere:
That predestination depends only on God's will. That he has elected those he has willed by an entirely gratuitous mercy.

Ibid.: *As the gift of grace is an effect of predestination, so also, in some way, hardening is an effect of eternal reprobation; but God does not harden, as Augustine says to Sixtus, by handing out evil, but rather by not handing out grace; it is said that God hardens them, not that he makes them sin but that he does not take pity on them; and he does not take pity on those to whom he has decided not to give grace by a righteousness very hidden and very distant from the human sense of righteousness, which the Apostle did not show us, but which he admired when he cried, "O height," and so on.*[16]

I think that the most blind see clearly, following the Master of the Sentences, that God predestined without foreseeing merits, and rejected some to whom he does not give his grace.

16. Pascal takes these quotations from Lombard from Arnauld, *Jansénius*, 306–7, where they appear in both Latin and French in the order Pascal gives them here.

PASCALIANISM RECONFIGURED[1]

The *Writings* contain a grammar of grace. A grammar is a lexicon with a syntax. Treatments of technical subjects such as grace typically deploy terms of art, more or less precisely defined, together with principles as to how they ought and ought not be combined. That is the grammar of the discourse, and skill in using it permits those who have it to recognize and make well- and ill-formed sentences and paragraphs belonging to the discourse. Pascal offers just such a grammar in the *Writings*, and my purpose here is to display it, affirming it where appropriate and criticizing it where necessary.

First, though, before treating Pascal's particular grammar of grace, some observations on the place and use of the word *grace* in Christian writing and talk more generally. In pre-Christian Latin, if something is *gratus* (adjective), it is charming, or pleasant, or delightful, or dear, and it gets to be that way by *gratia* (grace), for which it expresses, or should, *gratitudo* (gratitude) to the source from which the gifts that made it charming, and so on, came. The noun, *gratia*, can also be used in the other direction, to indicate the kindness, or gift, that made the one who is *gratus* grateful.

From that web of reciprocity comes the standard Latin locution *gratias agere*, which means to give thanks—typically to someone for something. To be a recipient or donor of *gratia*, then, is to enter into the

---

1. The remarks that follow treat Pascal as someone to recapitulate and argue with, and they take 'Pascal' to mean just and only the words of the *Writings*. They therefore avoid the following topics: placement of Pascal's treatment of grace in the terrain of seventeenth-century French analyses of the topic; placement of the *Writings* within the context of Pascal's *oeuvre* as a whole; assessment of the adequacy or accuracy of Pascal's use of his sources; analysis of Pascal's originality as theorist of grace. These are all important topics, but they are outside my concern here.

economy of gift and gratitude, and to be made beautiful (charmed and charming) by so doing. There is the beginning of a nexus here among gift, order, and beauty: to be *gratus* is to be beautifully ordered by way of gift, cosmeticized like the cosmos (that is Greek, but the pattern of thought is the same), which requires some artifice and can only be properly received as gift.

Another standard use of *gratia* in Latin is instructive: when *gratia* is used in the ablative and linked to a noun in the genitive, the meaning is *for the sake of, for the benefit of, out of consideration for*, and the like—as in the tag *ars gratia artis*, art for art's sake. Such a usage indicates that *gratia*'s grammar is fundamentally relational and essentially beneficial: *x* gives *y gratia* for *y*'s good, and *y*'s receipt of *gratia* (given *gratis*, ideally, of course) makes *y gratus*—charmingly and charmedly gifted and grateful.

There is nothing especially Christian in all that. The grammar of grace in English, rooted as it partly is in this pre-Christian Latin field of meaning, cannot be considered without attending to the specifically Christian use of the word (*gratia*, that is, and its calques in the European vernaculars—*grazia, grâce, grace, gracia, Gnade*, and so on). Briefly on that, and limiting ourselves now to English as inheritor of the western (that is, Latin) as distinct from the eastern (that is, Greek) Christian tradition, we can say the following.

Grace is a gift that God gives to us. It is what God is to us. It is a gift in the sense that we do not merit it (deserve it), and have, therefore, no right to expect it. It is a gift, too, in the sense that what it gives is available to us only by gift: we have no other way of getting it than to receive it from a donor other than ourselves. Like life. Like kisses. Like conversation. Grace's purpose is to bring its recipients to endless and indefectible intimacy with its giver—with God, that is. Grace opens that possibility to us, a possibility that would otherwise be closed. The content of the gift is also its giver. What God gives is God, at least to the extent that we can receive that gift. Only that gift, the gift of a lover by that same lover to a beloved, can bring about its purpose, which is, again, intimacy with the lover.

Grace is not given to all equally, nor is it found identically everywhere. It is a matter of rough ground. There are places (timespaces) where grace pools and accumulates (the incarnation of Christ, and the sacraments that derive from it; Mary, as *gratia plena*; wherever an act of love is done); and there are places of devastation, where it is largely, (but never entirely), absent.

Grace is compatible with freedom. Christians say that the gift is freely received, which is the same as to say that its reception and use are not compelled. Cooperation is one trope for this; concurrence another; participation a third; and there are more. Those tropes are intended to hold together God's action in giving and ours in receiving, neither of which, according to Christianity's grammar, can be fully subsumed into the other. How to hold the affirmation of the priority of the gift to its reception together with the affirmation of the necessity of the gift's free reception is one of the neuralgic points of tension within Christianity.

That is grace's fundamental Christian grammar in the European vernaculars. Pascal assumes it. His particular contributions are made within its ambit.

Grace and Delight

Grâce, for Pascal, in all its kinds (I will return to these), is a kind of help (*secours*). To get grace, to be graced, is to get help. But help with what and for what? For Pascal, the help is with entering upon the Christian life and then persevering in that life; and the content of the gift which makes those things possible is delight. Those to whom grace is given, for as long as it is given, (there is never, for Pascal, any guarantee short of heaven that grace, once given, may not be withdrawn), become lovers of the good, and therefore of God, and therefore behave toward God as lovers do, wanting to please the beloved in everything, and finding it delightful, and therefore easy, to do so. What the beloved wants is what the lover delights in giving. Pascal likes the Augustinian tag that the Christian life *n'est autre chose qu'un saint désir* (§1), and that desire is inflamed by grace.

The only way in which the Christian life may be lived is by finding it delightful—"when he <Augustine> says the commandments are not impossible, he intends it in the sense that they are not impossible for love (*ils ne sont pas impossibles à la charité*), which can be scattered in the heart by the Holy Spirit" (§10). Or, more technically:

We are now slaves to delight; what delights us more attracts us unfailingly. That is a principle so clear both to common sense and to St. Augustine that it cannot be denied without renouncing both of them. For what is clearer than the proposition that we always do what delights us most? That is nothing other than to say that we always do what pleases us most, which is to say that we always want what pleases us, which is to say that we always want what we want, and that in the state to which our souls are now reduced, it is inconceivable that they should want anything other than what it pleases them to want, which is to say what delights them most. We should not think to be subtle by saying that the will, in order to show its power, sometimes chooses what pleases it less. For in that case, it pleases it more to show its power than to will the good it leaves, so that when it forces itself to shun what pleases it, it is only to pursue what pleases it, it being impossible that it should want anything other than what pleases it to want. This caused the following maxim to be established by St. Augustine as fundamental to the way the will works: *Quod amplius delectat, secundum id operemur necesse est*[2]—it is necessary that we work in accord with what delights us most....That is how we are today slaves to delight. We unfailingly follow enslavement to flesh or spirit, and are freed from one only by the domination of the other. (§8)

Délectation (delight) is *plaisir* (pleasure) intensified. Since the Fall, anyway (the passage quoted is firmly located within a discussion of what life is like now, in the seventeenth, or twenty-first, century), human life is inevitably a matter of enslavement motivated by delight-inflected desire. We move toward what we want, which is, definitionally, what delights us, and we do so ineluctably, without any possibility of doing otherwise—*dans l'état où est aujourd'hui notre âme réduite, il est inconcevable*—that is, it would make no sense at all—*qu'elle veuille autre chose que ce qu'il lui plaît vouloir, c'est-à-dire, ce qui la délecte le plus.* If this is so, (a good case can be made for it), it is true also of those constrained by sheerly external forces—those physically enslaved as chattel, those incarcerated, those otherwise bound. They too, although unable to do what delights them, would if they could.

Pascal here makes a substantive claim, not merely one about the meanings of the words he uses. Yes, it is true that *on veut toujours ce que l'on veut*, which sounds neither substantive nor interesting; but the claim is that there is nothing else about us—not reason, certainly—capable of

---

2. Augustine, *Expositio* 49; Pascal's immediate source is unclear, but perhaps Jansenius, *Augustinus*, 3.4.6, col. 412.

leading us to action. We act, *post lapsum*, always and only in the service of desire, and desire is always and only a matter of delight, of pleasure, of what tickles (*chatouiller*) our fancy. We move toward those things as iron toward a magnet or plants toward the sun. We are, to seeking them, as an emerald is to greenness.

With that picture in mind, it is evident that grace, for Pascal, must, if it is to move its recipients to action, give one fundamental and essential thing: delight in itself and in its giver, which over time reconfigures desire so that what pleases God is the only force that motivates the lives of the graced. This means that the graced, those whose freedom, their *libre arbitre*, has been inflamed so that it *choisit infailliblement* (I will return to that adverb) *lui-même la Loi de Dieu par cette seule raison qu'il y trouve plus de satisfaction et qu'il y sent sa béatitude et sa félicité* (§11). This emphasis on desire-delight is central to the *Writings*. It is remarkable that almost every excerpt in the flower-garland of texts from late-antique and medieval Christian sources that makes up §13 is about delight (*délectation*). It is as if Pascal selected the texts there with just that theme in mind.

Delight, then, is what grace gives. The gift of delight has wanting more of the same as its first consequence and acting so as to get it as its second. That gift is given with the purpose of salvation, and if, once you have received it, typically in baptism, you are lucky enough to continue getting it until death, then you are one of the *élus*, the elect, which is to say that you will persevere in the Christian life until the end because it delights you to do so. And it is exactly grace, acting as necessary and sufficient condition, that makes you such that you so delight and, therefore, so act: "Who does not know that < . . . > all the elect, which is to say all who persevere, do so by a grace that invincibly (*invinciblement*, another adverb like *infailliblement*) makes it so that they do, and without which they would not be able to?" (§9).

This idea, that grace works infallibly and invincibly upon those who get it, is one of Pascal's central claims about grace, and one of the central difficulties in what he writes about it. I will return to it, but before doing so, it is necessary to nuance the claim by adverting to what Pascal writes about the varieties in which grace comes (sufficient and effective), the way in which these work in the course of a human life (rectification and desertion), and the way in which they have worked during the history of the human race, from Adam to ourselves.

Grace Sufficient and Grace Effective[3]

Sufficient grace (*grâce suffisante*) looks at first glance as if it would be grace that suffices to bring about its results, as citizenship grants eligibility to vote in the political economy of the USA, or as baptism grants membership in Christ's body in the Christian economy. That is how sufficient conditions ordinarily work: when they obtain, their result inevitably—ineluctably, infallibly—also does. It is easy to read Pascal on *grâce suffisante* like this. But it is incorrect. When he glosses the phrase, he makes it clear that *sufficient* means *enough*, as here: "God gave Adam sufficient grace, which is to say grace in addition to which nothing else was necessary for accomplishing the precepts and remaining in righteousness" (§11). Notice the phrase, *nécessaire pour accomplir les préceptes*. Sufficient grace is a condition necessary, sine qua non, for its result, but not one that guarantees its result; when you have it, you have what you need, but no more. The sentence just quoted is about Adam's condition before the Fall, and this is typically the context in which Pascal uses the phrase *grâce suffisante* (or its equivalent, *secours suffisant*). From Pascal's point of view, which he calls Augustinian, sufficient grace—enough to make the Christian life possible, though never to guarantee it—is never given, and so cannot be had, since the Fall.

3. These two kinds of grace—*efficace* and *suffisante*—are clearly distinguished from one another, and the distinction between them is much used. Pascal does, in the *Writings*, occasionally identify other kinds of grace: *grâce discernante* (discriminating grace, for example in §7, Le Guern, *Oeuvres*, 2:260), which is the grace by means of which God would discriminate and separate those worth saving from those not, were that to be the way things work, and *grâce sanctifiante* (sanctifying grace, for example in §4, Le Guern, *Oeuvres*, 2:238), which would be the grace God uses to bring the elect to sanctity. But Pascal is not committed to these phrases as terms of art; they never become significant for him. And that is consistent with the thought that he is not committed to positions on the ontology of kinds of grace as many of his contemporaries and opponents were, but rather to grace's grammar: to deploying talk about kinds of grace when suggestive and useful, and dropping them when not. Distinctions among kinds of grace for the Pascal of the *Writings* are like distinctions among kinds of rain for meteorologists.

It is the Molinists who think it is given and can be had *post lapsum*, and Pascal, in §15, excoriates them for it. That they affirm its *post lapsum* possibility shows that they do not take seriously the damage done by the Fall to our patterns of desire and delight. We cannot now, for Pascal, be in a condition in which we can take or leave the Christian life, which is where receipt of *grâce suffisante/secours suffisant* would place us. We are too damaged for that.

Pascal shows awareness that there are other ways of using *suffisant*, whether applied to *grâce* or *secours*, including uses that make *secours suffisant* indicate something that would, if you had it, bring you ineluctably to salvation. When it is used in that way, it approaches what he prefers to call *grâce efficace*, or effective grace. He accepts that there is grace of that kind, grace that does its work infallibly; and is consistent in denying that such grace is given to all, and in preferring not to call it *grâce suffisante*.

To get clear on some of the twists and turns here, it is worth attending to the shape of §8, and in particular to the more knotty passages in it. It begins with discussion of the double desertion (*double délaissement*). In one of these desertions, God deserts (leaves, abandons, departs from) us first, and does so by withdrawing from those deserted the grace they would need in order to persevere in faith, in prayer, in keeping the commandments, and, in general, in what belongs to the Christian life. Here is Pascal's first attempt in §8 at stating the relation between *grâce efficace* and prayer, which latter here stands as synecdoche for the Christian life:

<if> all who actually pray do so by way of effective grace, and none among those who do not actually pray are unobstructedly able to do so, the question is surely resolved. Does it not follow necessarily that for as long as the righteous pray they are effectively helped, and that they do not cease praying so long as this effective help remains with them, and that when they do cease, they lack unobstructed ability to pray? Consequently, God has left them first, I do not say with no help, but without unobstructed help. (§8)

Prayer—*prière actuelle*, the very act—requires effective grace or effective help, which are, in this passage, the same. If you have these, then your ability to pray is unobstructed, which is to say that nothing stands between you and prayer. So long as you pray, you have *grâce efficace* to do so; that is the only way in which unobstructed capacity for the Christian life is possible at all. And when you stop praying, it is because you no longer have the grace to do so—which is to say that God has withdrawn from you, left you, deserted you, and done so first, with initiative. All this makes *grâce efficace* both necessary for the Christian life (sine qua non), and, when present, a guarantee of it. This guarantee is put in terms of lack or absence of obstruction for the living of that life: there is *pouvoir prochain* (unobstructed ability) and *secours prochain* (unobstructed help) when effective grace is given. Or, put differently but with the same conceptual content, unobstructed ability is what effective grace gives. Pascal does not at this place enter into further analysis of how it is that we exercise this unobstructed ability to live as Christians when effective grace provides it for us. That is a form of the broader question about the relation between God's agency and ours, which he discusses elsewhere in the *Writings*, and to which I return below.

Pascal appears not quite satisfied, however, with the formulation just quoted, and he follows it at once in §8 with another, congruent with the first but not identical with it. This is one of many instances in the *Writings* of a stutter: a formulation is given; a momentary silence falls because the tongue—the pen—has hung fire, caught up by the inadequacy of what has just been written; and then the pen picks up again, reprising and extending and altering the texture of the first thought:

we only pray by a grace that brings prayer about. Perhaps you will deny this;—that although all the righteous have grace sufficient for prayer, it nonetheless happens that no one prays except by way of effective grace, and so, although prayer does not happen for anyone unless produced by grace, the ability to pray is, nonetheless, found in all the righteous. But that is not tenable. It is a question of fact whether any among the righteous diminish their unobstructed ability to pray by what they do; that question can only be answered by information about all the righteous, specifically about how prayer takes shape among them. This means that it would be rash beyond relevance to be certain that prayer never fails to occur among the righteous, past and future, because of a diminution in their unobstructed ability produced by what they do. We cannot say the same about the Thomists' sufficient grace; that is to say that we can, without irrelevance, say that it is never diminished by what we do because the Thomists do not establish it as unobstructedly sufficient. But if this claimed ability of the righteous to pray is unobstructed, it is not possible to say with confidence that not all those who pray do so by way of this un-obstructed ability, but instead do so by way of effective grace. The upshot is that if St. Augustine and all the Fathers affirm that prayer is always a result of effective grace, it necessarily follows from such a universal claim that those who do not pray are not unobstructedly able to do so. (§8)

Pascal canvasses here the view of an objector, (*peut-être direz vous que non*), to the idea that prayer occurs only by way of effective grace, and it is instructive to see what the objector's view is, for it makes the shape of Pascal's preferred view clearer than it would otherwise be. The objector says that maybe it is possible to hold together the view that all the righteous (*les justes*—here, as typically, this means the baptized, those who have been rectified—*justifié*—by that sacramental act, and are as a result participants in righteousness—*justice*) have grace suffi-cient for prayer with the claim—an empirical claim—that nevertheless, none among the righteous prays by way of anything other than effective grace (*il n'arrive néanmoins que pas un ne prie que par une grâce effi-cace*). The negatives rather pile up here, but the point is clear enough: all prayer is *de facto* caused by effective grace, but *de jure* all the bap-tized have grace enough to do it anyway. That is the same as to say that all the baptized have unobstructed ability (*pouvoir prochain*) to pray. It is as though, on this objector's view, all the baptized are lying in bed half-awake in the morning, perfectly capable of getting up; but that as a contingent matter of fact, none of them does get up until they smell the coffee brewing. They have *grâce suffisante* and *pouvoir prochain* for getting out of bed; but *de facto* it is only the *grâce efficace* of the smell of the coffee that gets any of them out of bed.

Pascal finds this view unconvincing. It makes, he writes, the ques-tion of whether Christian life is lived by (in response to) effective grace one of empirically-ascertainable fact. It does this because it leaves open the possibility that some among the baptized might fail to pray, not because they did not get effective grace to do so, but instead because they have diminished (reduced, made ineffective) the *grâce suffisante* they already had by something they have done (or not done), which is the same as to reduce their *pouvoir prochain qu'il a de prier*—the un-obstructed ability they have to pray. Some among the baptized might fail to get out of bed in the morning, not because there is no coffee being made (i.e., not because *grâce efficace* is absent), but because they have become so habituated to laziness that getting up at sunrise is no longer possible for them. The objector's view, that is, leaves open the possibility that failure to persevere in the Christian life is due to something about the one who fails, and not to something about the one who gives grace.

This is not a position that can be accommodated into Pascal's version of Augustinianism, as he clearly writes at the end of the quotation under discussion. Having unobstructed ability to live the Christian life means, lexically and conceptually, being able to live that life without effective grace, which is, as Pascal sees it, a rejection of the entire Augustinian package. The objector shares with all anti-Augustinians a desire to sequester some part of us, (a capacity, a desire, an ability, a freedom, a nature), from grace's inflaming fire, and this means that we could fail all by ourselves, without God having anything to do with it.

A final comment on the excerpt just quoted. In it, Pascal affirms that some versions of *grâce suffisante* (he mentions the Thomists), do not fall foul of the Augustinian requirement that effective grace is necessary for the Christian life. They do not do that because whatever they mean by *sufficient*, it is not *unobstructedly sufficient*. Were the adverbial modifier present, it would imply that those who had such grace were placed by it in a condition without barriers of distance between them and the practice of the Christian life, which would be, like the objector, to remove effective grace's necessity for that life. *Grâce suffisante*, then, can be affirmed within the ambit of Augustinianism, just so long as it does not guarantee that we are able to live the Christian life without something more, some particular help, a help that Pascal most often calls *grâce efficace*.

A little further on in §8, Pascal writes:

All who persevere in prayer have effective grace, which makes it so that they both pray and persevere in prayer; and that all those who have that grace pray; while those who do not persevere in prayer are destitute of that effective grace, and of grace unobstructedly sufficient; and that those destitute of that sufficient grace do not pray; so that none among the righteous cease to pray unless their doing so follows upon God's making them destitute of the effective grace unobstructedly sufficient for prayer. (§8)

This makes it entirely clear, if any further clarity were needed, that for Pascal *grâce efficace* is both necessary for its outcome and guarantees that outcome. If you have it and keep it, both states of affairs being solely within God's gift and at God's discretion, you will persevere in the Christian life; without it, you will not live that life.

Double Desertion

Some further clarity about the workings of grace as Pascal sees them can be had by looking in more detail at what he writes about *délaissement* (desertion): God's of us, ours of God:

St. Augustine does not contradict himself when, having established by all his principles that grace is so effective and so necessary that we never leave God if God has not first left us without this help, so that, for as long as it pleases God to retain us, we never separate ourselves from him; he does not avoid saying in some places that God does not leave those among the righteous who have not left him. These two states of affairs subsist together because of their different senses. For God does not cease giving help to those who do not cease asking for it. But also, we would not cease asking for it if God had not ceased giving us grace to ask for it, so that, with respect to this double cessation, God always commences one, and never the other. (§12)

Pascal here reaffirms that grace guarantees its effects: *tant qu'il lui* <God> *plaît de le* <the recipient of grace> *retenir, l'homme ne s'en separe jamais*—so long as we are graced (with effective grace), we do not, because we cannot, separate ourselves from the one who dazzles us with grace's delights. But nevertheless, separation happens. Not all the righteous-baptized remain with God, living the Christian life. (Pascal takes this to be obvious). How does that happen? At the level of logic, and in the order of time, God leaves first: if *grâce efficace* is both necessary for and a guarantee of perseverance in Christian life, and if its gift is solely at God's will, then it follows at once that anyone who lives the Christian life for a while and then ceases to do so can only do that, can only cease, because God withdraws effective grace. That is the first desertion: God's of us.

The second desertion, ours of God, is shown in this treatment by Pascal of an excerpt from Augustine's *De correptione et gratia*:

St. Augustine <…> treats the same thing with the same clarity when, in discussing generally the fall of all the reprobate who came to righteousness for a time, he says <…> *they receive grace for a time; they leave and are left; for they have been abandoned to their free choice by a righteous but hidden judgment*—from this it is evident that we leave and then are left; that is the desertion in which God follows, in which there is nothing mysterious. But if we ask why they leave, St. Augustine gives the reason that *they have been abandoned to their free choice*. They are, therefore, abandoned before leaving, and, further, they leave only because they are left. That is the desertion that God commences, and it is done by a hidden and impenetrable judgment. (§12)

The reprobate (*réprouvés*) who come to righteousness for a time (*qui arrivent pour un temps à la justification*) are the baptized who do not persevere in the Christian life. They desert or leave God exactly by not continuing in that life, and that is the desertion in which what we do comes first and what God does comes second. But why do we leave? Why do we, for example, cease to pray? Only because, in Augustine's words, *dimissi enim sunt libero arbitrio*, which Pascal renders as *car ils ont été abandonnés à leur libéral arbitre*. They have been abandoned to freedom, or more exactly to the freedom of choice, and that is why they give up the Christian life. Our desertion, then, is made possible only by God's, which is as it should be if *grâce efficace* is both necessary for and a guarantee of the Christian life. It is worth noting, too, that both Augustine and Pascal here locate talk of freedom firmly within the context of talk about falling and failing: falling and freedom go together syntactically as tightly as do grace and election. This, too, is a matter to return to.

Fall and Election

The double desertion is Pascal's picture of how falling from grace works in the life of an individual Christian: we are baptized, and the effective grace we receive then rectifies us, or sets us straight: we are *justifié*, and we begin to live as Christians. When we fall from that graced life it is because God withdraws from us the grace that both makes it possible and guarantees it, and we then do the only thing possible for ungraced freedom (*post lapsum*, anyway), which is to fall. Falling (*tomber, chuter*) is what libertarian freedom—freedom unresponsive to God—does. It is a grammatical rule for Pascal that when free choice works freely in a libertarian sense, it must always be said to fall, just as when we act under and in response to *grâce efficace*, we can only ever be said to rise, to delight in God.

Pascal also paints a picture of the history of the human race with grace from Adam to ourselves, and the details of this confirm the sketch already given, although from a different angle. The story is this: Adam came from God's hand free, undamaged, and innocent, given by God all he needed to live as he ought—with, that is, *grâce suffisante et nécessaire pour accomplir les préceptes* (§11). Adam had what he needed to act well, but did not have *grâce efficace*, (that was on offer only after the Fall), and so he could freely choose whether to act well or badly. He was *également flexible au bien et au mal* (§11), in equilibrium, that is, between good and evil, capable of moving toward either (§8). Adam had, that is to say, an unobstructed ability or capacity, a *pouvoir prochain*, to move toward or live by either. It was up to him. He chose evil. He fell. Everything changed.

God had willed to save Adam, in Pascal's view, but with a *volonté conditionelle*, a will conditioned upon what Adam did. When Adam did the wrong thing, God left him to himself, and thereby *dans l'amour de la créature* (§11), in creaturely love, understood as both objective and subjective genitive—Adam, *post lapsum*, loves creatures and loves as creatures do. That kind of love—Pascal calls it concupiscence—becomes delightful for him, and he and all his descendants are enslaved to it, without the possibility of liberating themselves, and even without possibility of attenuating or moderating the attractiveness of those *délices* for themselves. All human creatures, then, form a *masse corrompue*, a corrupt mass, worthy of damnation, deserted by God. No *grâce efficace* here; no *grâce suffisante*, either; almost no grace at all. Just devastation.

God's response to this is to choose, to elect (*élire*), some for salvation, and to do that by giving them effective grace. Pascal's dominant metaphors for this election are those of distinction and separation. The elect (*élus*) are taken out of the corrupt mass, discerned, discriminated, and removed therefrom, inscrutably, and given grace so that they delight in God:

To save his elect, God sent Jesus Christ, to satisfy his righteousness, and to merit by his mercy the grace of redemption—medicinal grace, the grace of Jesus Christ, which is nothing other than sweetness and delight in God's law scattered in the heart by the Holy Spirit. That sweetness not only equals but surpasses even the flesh's concupiscence; it fills the will with a greater delight in good than concupiscence offers it in evil. And in that way free choice, charmed by the softnesses and the pleasures breathed into it by the Holy Spirit more than by sin's attractions, unfailingly chooses the law of God for the sole reason that it finds more satisfaction in it, and senses there its beatitude and its felicity. (§11)

This excerpt underscores again the importance of delight in the call of the elect. It is because they are given the gift of delight in it that they unfailingly (*infailliblement*) choose (*choisir*, a verb of volition) what God wants. Election is indefectible in two senses, then, or, perhaps better, in a single sense with two directions. That is, in election, God unfailingly gives delight; and when that delight is unfailingly received, the elect, its recipients, unfailingly act in accord with it by doing what it (now) pleases them to do. Since, as Pascal sees it, God never withdraws grace from the elect, and since the grace (*grâce efficace*, of course) given always and inevitably produces its result, which is the delighted gratitude of those who get it, their falling-away, their failure, can never happen.

The elect, for Pascal, are a minority, perhaps a tiny one, of humans: the elect are *peu à proportion de la totalité des délaissés* (§11), that is, few in proportion to the number of the abandoned, who are also the damned. It is axiomatic for him that most are damned, and that it would have been entirely just of God to leave everyone to damnation after the Fall. The elect are few in number, then, and we have no access to God's reasons for electing some rather than others. Here is a typical formulation:

Acknowledge frankly, therefore, the grandeur of this mystery: why one perseveres and another does not. In order to look at it in all its depth, you should clearly conceive that if God had willed to damn everyone, he would have exercised his righteousness; no mystery there. If he had effectively willed to save everyone, he would have exercised his mercy; no mystery there. And in willing to save some and not others, he has exercised both his mercy and his righteousness; no mystery there, either. But, when all are equally guilty, he has willed to save these and not those; there, properly, is the grandeur of the mystery. (§6)

The pattern of God's will is not mysterious to Pascal: he explains its shape with precision, a shape given by the relation between justice and mercy.

The form of that relation yields three possibilities with respect to the salvation and damnation of human creatures. God could mercifully have saved all; God could justly have damned all; and God could have saved some by election, and not others. As Pascal sees it, we know that the third possibility is actual, and that the first two are not; he takes this to be established beyond doubt by scriptural revelation and authoritative Church teaching. No mystery in any of this. What remains mysterious, *un secret absolument incompréhensible* (§9), is why some particular person is chosen, while some other person is not. Over that matter, a veil is cast.

That veil yields, for Pascal, an important conclusion: none of us can know whether we are ourselves among the elect, or whether any other living person is—that *on na jamais l'assurance de persévérer* (§6), no one ever has assurance of persevering in the Christian life. The distinction between the elect and the damned, then, is not reflected by any distinction apparent to us in the world we find ourselves in. And this epistemic limitation requires a rule of conduct:

Everyone is obliged to believe, though with a belief mixed with fear and unaccompanied by certitude, that they are among the small number of the elect whom Jesus Christ wills to save; and never to judge of any who live on the earth, however wicked and ungodly, so long as there remains to them a moment of life, that they are not among the number of the predestined, leaving the separation of the elect from the reprobate as God's impenetrable secret. This obliges everyone to do for all others what might contribute to their salvation. (§7)

This is Pascal's way of holding together two thoughts, each essential to his construal of the economy of grace. The first is that the number and identity of the elect can be known only to God and is established by God independently of anything we do; the second is that Christians must do what they can to live a Christian life themselves, and to bring others to do so. Why do the second, if the first is the case? If everyone now living either is or is not among the elect, then effort is useless to change that state of affairs in any particular case, including your own, and it might seem that Pascal's strenuous ideas about what belongs to the Christian life are eviscerated. Pascal's response to this apparent difficulty is to say, first, that while Christians have formal certitude about the economy of grace, about, that is, what grace is and how it works, they have none about which graces have been, are, or will be given to any particular person, including themselves. They must, therefore, pattern their lives in response to this combination of radical certitude about formalities and radical incertitude about particularities, and the Christian way to do that is by hope—or, as Pascal puts it in the excerpt quoted above, by way of fear-laced belief, which comes to the same thing. If Christians are to live a Christian life, and to encourage others to do the same, it cannot be because doing those things is an instrument that produces the gift of grace. But that does not mean there can be no reason, cause, or motive for living a Christian life.

If you are sure that your rich aunt's decision to leave you a fortune, or not to, will not and cannot be affected by whether you are nice to her, then if you are nice to her, it will not be because you think it will bring you a fortune. It might be because you like her and find being nice to her delightful; or because you are habituated to niceness toward elderly relatives; or because you think you have a duty to be nice to members of your family. There are other possibilities. Pascal has variants of these responses available to him. The most fundamental among them, for him, it seems, is the thought that grace produces delight in God. If, (and, of course, only if), you are given *grâce efficace*, you will live a Christian life and offer it to others because it seems delightful to you to do so. But it would also be possible for Pascal to say (although he does not, in the *Writings*), that Christians in the proper condition of uncertainty about whether they or anyone else among the living is elect, might live a Christian life and offer it to others because the Church tells them that it is right and just to do so, without respect to what it may do for them. A strict understanding, such as Pascal's, of the ineluctable power of grace and of the hidden nature of its particular workings need not, then, and in his case does not, yield anything like quietism.

This understanding of election assimilates God's choosing of the (Christian) elect to God's act of electing the Jewish people:

Because God engages himself by his promises to give to the children of the promise even if they do not ask him, he engages himself to give exactly to them the grace to pray to get the grace to live well; but since obligation always follows promise, God has it only to those he has made promises to—which is to say, the predestined. (§6)

Election involves promise. The structure of Christian thought about the election of the Jews is replicated in the way Pascal writes about the elect: God chooses Abraham over all others for reasons hidden from Abraham and us; the promise made to Abraham is unconditional and cannot be abrogated—no matter what Abraham's descendants think about it or do about it, it remains; it is nonetheless a good thing, an unsurpassably good thing, when the Jews delight in God and live as God would like them to. As Pascal puts it in the quotation above, *comme l'obligation n'est qu'en suite de sa promesse, il ne la doit qu'à ceux à qui il l'a promis*. And that means the elect. They are the chosen people.

This way of thinking about election, unsurprisingly, reduces the salvific significance of baptism and the other sacramental rites of the Church. Those rites give grace, for Pascal, of course—or, more exactly, they are the ordinary and paradigmatic way in which God has chosen to provide *grâce efficace* to their recipients. But those to whom such grace is given are not, and cannot be, coextensive with the elect. Were the two groups to be the same, then, first, the epistemic limitation just discussed would be removed. You would only have to find out whether someone (including yourself) was validly baptized to know whether they were elect; and, still more troublingly for Pascal, if baptism did indefectibly provide effective grace, and was known to do so, then certitude of salvation would begin to unpick the fabric of hope and fear that, as he sees it, are inevitable and proper concomitants of the Christian life. As here:

<If we had certitude of our own salvation> it would not only be fear that would be destroyed for them, but also hope, for as we do not hope for something certain, we also will not hope for the continuation of this help because it is certain for us; also, hope, for us, will not be to get what we ask for, because that too is certain. What then will be the object of our hope other than ourselves, for whom we hope good use of an ability of which we are assured? (§6)

Election's incertitude as Pascal presents it, removes self-reliance; certitude, if we could have it, would turn us back to ourselves. But a window opens here: if baptism, though it does guarantee at least temporary reception of *grâce efficace*, does not guarantee perseverance in that state of grace, then it is possible to say, without contradicting anything in Pascal's grammar of grace, that *grâce efficace* might be given outside the Church's sacramental economy, and that those who receive it in that way might, if it continues to be given, persevere to the end.

Concurrence

Pascal likes to use the vocabulary of freedom (*libre arbitre*; *choix/ choisir*) for what the elect do when they respond with delight to God's gift of effective grace. Here is a typical example:

Those to whom it pleases God to unfailingly give that grace move themselves by their free choice to prefer God to creatures. That is why it can equally well be said that free choice moves itself by way of that grace, because in effect it does move itself; or that grace moves free choice, because whenever grace is given free choice unfailingly follows. (§11)

The elect persevere unfailingly (inevitably, invincibly, necessarily), but they do so by choice. They are not *comme une pierre, comme une scie* (§11), inanimate objects in the hand of those who wield them. (Pascal presents the Calvinists as making that claim, and it is, he thinks, *abominable* and *épouvantable* (§7)). Rather they act intentionally, with volition, and thus freely, in response to and with God, even though, or just because, they must do so.

This is not a libertarian understanding of choice and freedom, according to which those who act freely could have done otherwise, being suspended uncommittedly between or among alternatives. If any human was ever free in this sense, for Pascal, it was Eve and Adam before the Fall. They had grace sufficient for doing good, but not grace effective for producing good action. For all others, since the Fall, we act freely for the good only when we act cooperatively or concurrently with what God does. As here:

All our good actions have two sources: our will, and God's <...> if we ask why adults are saved, we can rightly say that it is because they willed it so, and that it is because God willed it so. If one or the other had not so willed, it would not have happened. But even though these two causes have concurred to produce this result, there is nevertheless considerable difference in the concurrence of each. Our will is not the cause of God's, while God's is the cause, source, and principle of ours, working that will in us. The result is that although we can attribute actions either to our will or to God's, and the two causes seem to concur equally. Nevertheless, there is this thoroughgoing difference: we can attribute an action solely to God's will to the exclusion of ours; but that action cannot be attributed solely to our wills to the exclusion of God's. (§12)

Pascal here makes, first, a grammatical point. We can rightly say (*on a droit de dire*) that our will—what we want and seek—is involved when we act rightly; indeed, we must say that. Such assertions are a required and non-negotiable element of Christian grammar, and those who refuse them, as Pascal takes Calvinists and Lutherans to do, move outside that grammar and begin to speak a different language. Second, we can also rightly say that when we act well, God wills that we should. This assertion, and others like it, also belongs to Christian grammar, and in the same sense as assertions about human will and human freedom. There is a third family of claims required of Christians: it is that our will and God's will are not on a par. They do not work as zero-sum competitors on the same field, so that the extent to which one acts is the extent to which the other does not. Rather, God's will comes first, as *la cause et la source et le principe* of ours; ours then follows as second, derived from, dependent upon, and (so long as we are acting rightly), infallibly following God's. Christians can, in certain contexts and for certain purposes, say that it is God's will alone that works good in and for us. But Christians cannot, in any context or for any purpose, say that it is our will alone that performs the good we do. That, again, is a grammatical point: the asymmetry in the order of being between what we do and what God does is what requires the difference in the grammatical order between what can be said of God's will and of ours.

What language is available to Christians, then, for specifying the relation between our wills and God's when we are acting rightly? Both are active and efficacious; but they are not on a par; they do not oppose one another as zero-sum competitors. In the excerpt just above, Pascal's language for the relation is that of *concours*, or concurrence—running along together, we might say. When God acts by giving *grâce efficace*, something is set going, which is delight-based right action on the part of the recipient. That action is always responsive, and always dependent: it could not occur without being initiated by gift, and once it has been initiated, it cannot cease to occur. But it is not, Pascal wants Christians to learn to say, thereby reduced to nothing. Our characteristic mode of active response to the gift of grace is to interlock, or mesh, our response to God's gift, and then to act concurrently with God's action, for just as long as God continues to act. Just as, to use an analogy Pascal does not, but which is concordant with his thought, we cannot converse when our conversation-partner stops talking, but only soliloquize; so we cannot act rightly when God ceases giving us the grace to do so, but only deliberately fall back into the void whence we came—on which more below.

The fundamental mistake in Christian talk about God's agency and ours, Pascal's way of putting things suggests, is to construe our action and God's as competitive. Once that mistake is renounced, it is possible to look for, and find, language that affirms the prevenience of God's action and the reality of ours. Human freedom then becomes, definitionally, what we do when we respond, as we must, to grace.

One last example, following closely upon the preceding excerpt, of Pascal attempting language for the relation between God's action and ours, here drawing upon Paul's language from the Corinthian and Galatian correspondence:

For when we say that an action comes from our will, we consider human will as secondary cause, not as primary cause; when we look for the primary cause, we attribute the action to God's will alone and exclude it from ours. Accordingly, St. Paul, having said, *I have worked more than anyone*, adds *not me*, which is to say, *I have not worked, but his grace, which is with me, has done so*. This shows that he attributes his work to his own will, and that he refuses to do so, depending upon whether he looks for the secondary cause or the primary; but he never attributes it to himself alone, giving it instead to grace alone, and that it is when speaking correctly that he says he gives it to grace alone. In accord with this he says: *I live, not me, but Jesus Christ in me*. He says, *I live*, and adds, *I do not live*. It is true that life is his to the extent that he wants to mark the secondary cause, and that it is not his to the extent that he wants to mark the primary cause. (§12)

Paul, as Pascal here reads him, uses the language of primary and secondary cause for the same point made just now with the language of concurrence. God's will is primary and ours secondary, which permits us to affirm-and-deny that we act, as Paul does, but only to affirm that God acts. But the affirmation of our action is not simply removed, either by Paul or by Pascal. It remains, subordinate and responsive, but not absent. The blooming rose turns its face to the sun, which it could not do were there no sun, and which it unfailingly does when the sun shines. But this does not mean that it does nothing: its action remains, a responsive but real action. It does mean that the action could not be otherwise, and so if freedom is defined in such a way as to require that a free action must have been able to be otherwise in order to be free, then neither the plant's action nor, as Pascal sees it, human action under grace, are free. But if freedom means action in accord with one's kind and capacity in response to gift given, (sunshine, grace), then human action under grace is as free as freedom gets.

It should be remembered that, for Pascal, Adam was free in a way that we are not and cannot be. Adam, supported by *grâce suffisante*, could have chosen good or evil, and chose evil; we, since the fall, saved by *grâce efficace* or damned by its lack, have no such choice. If gifted, we freely respond; if not, we remain where we have always been, which is sunk irretrievably in corruption—damned, that is.

Pascal Reconfigured

Pascal's grammar of grace is a chain of concepts so tightly linked that were any of the connections broken, it might seem that all would be. Pascal often so presents it: there is effective grace, requisite for and guarantee of all the constituents of the Christian life (faith, prayer, good works, participation in the sacraments, and so on); as long as you have effective grace you will live that life, and without it you will not because you cannot. It follows at once that effective grace is required for and guarantees not only all the elements of that life, however they might be characterized, but also perseverance in it. Should you live the Christian life for a decade and then cease to do so, the only possible explanation for ceasing is that you no longer have effective grace. And if you begin again after a hiatus, the only possible explanation is that you temporarily lost effective grace, and then got it back. If anything at all about the Christian life (the beginning of faith, contrition for sin, delight in what God gives, love of neighbor, love of enemy, and so on) is sequestered from what effective grace does, the entire picture blows away like a sand mandala at the end of its life. Christian life is a matter of grace from beginning to end. No element of it is ours.

If there were some element or aspect or precondition of Christian life that you could undertake or persevere in outside the economy of grace, (within, say, the economy of nature; or that of libertarian freedom), that would have to mean that you are capable of acting independently of God. And the grammar of Christianity does not permit that view for the same reason that it does not permit the view that there can be anything at all not made by God. Both views, or, better, both families of views, try to sequester something from grace, which is to say from God. Were there something (prime matter? sin? evil?) God had not made, the immediate entailment would be that God is not God—because the God of Abraham, Isaac, Jacob, and Jesus is the one who brought everything other than Godself into being out of nothing, and if there are things not so made, then there is no God like that. When Christians speak or write of things not made by God, and when they also ask what the status of those putative things is, the answer is and must be always the same: such things are not; they are privations, absences, lacks, nothings for which there is neither time nor space.

Just so with human action. Attempts to find a place for something we do by and for ourselves fail for the same reason that brings failure to attempts to find a place for things God did not make. There are no such places. All that we do is and must be, by way of concurrence (Pascal's preferred word in the *Writings*) with or participation (as I would prefer to say), in what God does. Speaking of grace as effective in Pascalian mode guarantees that conclusion because it makes impossible the sequestration of any human actions from God's action. So far with Pascal.

But there is then an obvious question. According to Pascal, were not Eve and Adam in a position of flexible equilibrium between good and evil? Could they not, because they had been given only *grâce suffisante* and not *grâce efficace*, act in opposition to God by sinning, and do so by themselves, unobstructedly and without help? Did they not in fact do so? And does not so saying invalidate the claim just made, which is that no human action is sequestrable from the economy of grace, that there is nothing we humans can do by and for ourselves? Should not Christians sequester at least sinful action?

Yes and no.

Sin, the free choice of evil for evil's sake, which is what sin always is at bottom and in its purity, exactly is something we can do for and by ourselves. We certainly do not and cannot do it by concurring with *grâce efficace*. That is the yes. But the no undercuts the yes. What we do when we sin is nothing: it is an act—better, an anti-act, related to acts properly speaking as self-starvation is to eating, or cutting one's tongue out is to speaking (imperfect but illustrative analogies). Sin is sequestered from grace, but that is only because it does not amount to an action, or indeed to anything. That is the no. Love of and desire for evil is love of and desire for nothing, and putting matters in that way does not require any modification of Pascalianism.

There is, however, another difference between Adam and us if we follow the *Writings*, a difference additional to the possibility of embracing the lack that is evil. It is that Adam and Eve could, as Pascal sees things, have delighted in and embraced God—have continued, that is, in the condition in which they were made—*juste, sain, fort* as Pascal writes of Adam—without *grâce efficace* (§11). The grace they had, *grâce suffisante*, gave them the *pouvoir*, the ability unobstructedly (*prochainement*) to do the good. This, in the end, amounts to a rejection of the axiomatic commitment to non-sequestration of human agency through the lens by which I have so far been interpreting Pascalianism. It amounts to that because it permits Eve and Adam a capacity to delight in God because of what they are, which is what they have been made to be, without grace that guarantees they will do so. Eve and Adam become angelic in respect of the relation of their wills to grace. Pascal is aware of this. The reconfiguration of Pascalianism I am about to recommend will entail a rejection of this difference between them and us, but a fuller presentation of the reasons should wait upon a delineation of the other significant difference between Pascal's Pascalianism and the version I prefer.

The *Writings* often present *grâce efficace* as though its effects upon those who receive it are immediate—like a dam breaking and irresistibly inundating the valley below with delight and all its associated goods. It is not difficult to reconfigure Pascalianism so as to modify that impression, and in a way entirely consistent with his grammar. God gives *grâce efficace* as requisite for and guarantee of the Christian life, we may agree; but because not every recipient is in the same condition, the results do not always occur with the same rapidity, or with the same smoothness when they do begin to occur. *Post lapsum*, recall, we are all concupiscent, slaves to sin, bedazzled by evil. But slavery and bedazzlement may take different forms and perhaps work at different intensities, some of which respond gradually to grace, exhibiting incremental change over a long period, while others exhibit no change at all for a time, and then, suddenly and all at once, precipitously abandon one slavemaster for the other. The eventual result is the same, as it must be if *grâce efficace* is both requisite for and a guarantee of perseverance. But there is no reason, within the constraints of Pascalianism, to expect the perceptible trajectory toward that eventual result always to be the same.

That is a friendly amendment to the *Writings* rather than an overturning of anything in them. It sits well, too, with Pascal's frequent emphasis on and occasional depiction of backsliding. *Les justes*, the righteous, rectified by baptism, often do cease to live the Christian life, and may, as he sees it, persevere in this cessation until they are damned. Pascal attributes these failures to God's mysterious withdrawals of grace, and it is consistent with his understanding of God, and of *grâce efficace*, and of us, to do so. This means, among other things, that it is difficult, probably impossible, to say that baptized persons not among the elect, are, in any way other than having been conceived and born, responsible for their damnation. But there is nothing in Pascalianism to rule out other, additional, explanations of the temporal unevenness with which grace seems to work.

There is, however, one aspect of the grammar of grace in the *Writings* that should be not just reconfigured, but overturned. I mean the claim that, *post lapsum*, God inscrutably separates the few elect from the corrupt mass of the damned, floods the elect with *grâce efficace* in such a way as to make their perseverance inevitable, and gives grace to the non-elect, if at all, only temporarily, withdrawing it if given in such a way as to ensure the damnation of all the non-elect. This assumption is additional to the connections Pascal sets up to relate and order the central terms of his grammar. Its detachment leaves unscathed the relation he proposes between *grâce efficace* and perseverance, and between our action and God's. The assumption also leaves untouched, therefore, Pascal's main polemical point in the *Écrits*, which is the refusal of sequestration. It does, though, open some horizons for theological thought that are closed to Pascal, and it does that retrospectively, by reordering thought about the similarities and differences between Adam and us; and prospectively, by doing the same about the scope of salvation.

Here is how the picture can be repainted, by way of a close calque on §11:

God made Eve and Adam from nothing, straight and right and sound and free, immortal and undamaged, unbedazzled by evil or by good.

God gave them *grâce efficace*, grace that would eventually save them, but that would permit them, should they so will, to reject it and its giver for a time, even though God had *volonté absolue* to save them and with them, all their offspring.

Eve and Adam, like the fallen angels, did reject the grace given them, without apparent cause. They fell, and were damaged. They became mortal, subject to pain, violently concupiscent, fearful, moved irresistibly by the empty glamour of evil's lack. The same for all their descendants after them.

God withdrew *grâce efficace* from no one, not from Eve and Adam, and not from any of their descendants. Rather, by way of election (for Jews) and baptism (for Christians), and in other ways unknown, God renewed that grace, making it beautiful to the purblind, luring and encouraging and seducing and soothing and demanding and complaining and scolding and threatening until some turned to what was being offered them, and said yes, oh yes—a turning that was itself a work of the grace offered, a turning for which that grace was requisite and guarantee.

But most die in pain and fear, even so; most spend their lives deepening the damage to which they have been made unwillingly subject; most unmake themselves by grasping what cannot be had. And for those who die unready for God, there is more suffering, purgatorial when accepted, hellish when not, but almost always intense and long.

Even then, *grâce efficace* is not removed. The offer is always made. And God finds a way, often a way that takes much time, to make it so that even the most damaged, diminished, and agonized, at last, by the end, find the offer—an offer that contains nothing except the one making it—beautiful, and are delighted by it.

And at last, all concur with God and act by grace in a movement of love. As they always would. Eve and Adam and all their descendants are lifted from the pit by the fringes of Abraham's shawl and the fingers of the resurrected Jesus. The fallen angels too, at last, turn back to God, in ways opaque to us but necessary for the economy of grace. God, in the end, delights them too, and when their long sojourn in purgatory comes to an end and the resurrection of all for salvation has been effected, there is only a delighted peace.

That is Pascal's grammar with two exceptions. The first is about God. For Pascal God has, prior to the Fall, a conditional will to save all humans, and, after the Fall, an absolute will to save some among them, which means that only some, eventually, are saved. In this revised version, God has only an absolute will to save all, which means that all, eventually, are saved. The second is about us. For Pascal, Eve and Adam are different from us in two ways: they are not damaged, and they are given grace enough, *grâce suffisante*, but not what we get, which is *grâce efficace*, grace that guarantees.

In this revised version, Eve and Adam are different from us only in the first way: they fall even without prior damage, whereas our sins and backslidings are always in the context of damage already present. Their fall is like that of the angels: a surd to which cause cannot be attributed, but not less real for that. Ours is more comprehensible. Because our desires are already bent toward evil, that we follow them is not puzzling. Even Christians (the baptized, the rectified) are not, by their baptisms, made angelic or adamic. Their pre-baptismal damage has effects upon their post-baptismal life, which is why the churches have sacramental means at their disposal for rectifying post-baptismal sin.

Pascal's explanation for post-baptismal sin is that God withdraws *grâce efficace*, temporarily or permanently, from those among the baptized who sin. In the revised version, such withdrawals do not happen. It is definitional of God that they do not. All grace is effective, finally, and is never withdrawn. To say that it is, or that it could be, is a solecism of the same order as the sequestration of some good actions from the reach of grace. Pascal recognizes and excoriates solecisms of that kind; he should, (and could, without incoherence), do the same for this one. If the baptized are photosynthesizing plants, God the sun, and the Church the gardener, then the gardener's work (the sacraments) removes barriers between the plants and the sun, straightens them, and gives them nourishing soil in which to grow. All the while, the sun shines, unremittingly and freely. But the root systems are frail, still; the plants droop, sometimes, seeking the darkness they have been removed from—sinning again, that is. The sun, however, is not withdrawn. When they turn to it again, as they will, it is there; and the Church, meanwhile, works unremittingly, before and after their deaths, to help them make that turn and to grow straight, so that they may soak up the sun.

All this applies as much to Eve and Adam, once fallen, as to their descendants, Christian and otherwise. (It would be a longer discussion, for which this is not the place, to consider how it is that God encourages those altogether outside the sanctifying presence of Israel or the Church to turn toward the sun.) The fundamental and essential difference between this revised Pascalianism and the positions taken in the *Writings* is that God, because of the universal salvific will, never deserts any of us; and our desertions of God, though real and commonplace, are always temporary. There are no elect as Pascal understands the word, again because of the universal salvific will; though there are elect in the sense that the economy of grace in a devastated world is rough rather than smooth; and that roughness is evident principally in the call of Abraham and the incarnation of Jesus.

Everything else remains the same. There is no sequestration: we do nothing good without grace, and when we are given grace we do, and must, eventually respond to it. Grace works, first and last, by delight. When we respond to it, we do so because it is delightful, and because it seems, however gradually and painfully and burningly, delightful to us.

And each of us should hope that we are among those now responding rightly to grace, and that none of those we encounter is among those continuing to refuse grace by nonaction. Even fear survives, sadly: we are damaged enough that we often cannot tell which among the actions we contemplate and perform deepen our damage, and which lessen it. We need not fear, as Pascal would have us do, that we may fall and fail irremediably. But we should fear that what we do we may make matters worse for ourselves and others for a long time to come, and bring wide and deep suffering with it. That is as much fear as we need or can live with.

This revised version works, then, within the constraints of Pascalianism, which is also Augustinianism in all the most fundamental ways, and it, like the Pascalianism of the *Writings*, numbers Calvinism and Molinism among its enemies. If Molinism is characterized as Pascal does, as an accommodation to common sense that makes our salvation depend, finally, on us rather than on God, then this revised version is not that. And if Calvinism is characterized as Pascal does, as a rebarbative attribution to God of an absolute will for damnation independent of us, then this revised version is not that either.

This revised Pascalianism, like the position taken in the *Writings*, sees our agency and God's as inextricably linked, concurrent and participatory; and it sees that grace, in order to be grace, must in the end and in the beginning be effective. The revised version is a fourth option, not considered by Pascal because he takes it to be obvious that some are damned, and the only way to achieve that end, given his understanding of *grâce efficace*, is to attribute that outcome to God's *post lapsum* absolute will. It is instructive that Pascal does not, in the *Writings*, argue for the position that some are damned; that is mostly because he was not faced with anyone, Catholic or Protestant, who thought otherwise. And if that axiom is detached from his grammar of grace, almost everything survives, and certainly everything of worth. It is among the benefits of reading Pascal on grace that the clarity and energy of his prose makes that conclusion abundantly clear.

The Council of Trent on Keeping
the Commandments[1]

(from the Prooemium)

<The Council> intends to set out for all the Christian faithful the true and sound doctrine of rectification, which Jesus Christ, the sun of righteousness,[2] author and perfecter of our faith,[3] taught, the apostles handed on, and the Catholic Church, prompted by the Holy Spirit, has always retained; the Council strictly forbids that anyone henceforward dare believe, preach, or teach otherwise than is established and declared in this decree.

Chapter XI—The Keeping of the Commandments: Its Necessity and Possibility

None, however much rectified, ought consider themselves exempt from keeping the commandments, or deploy the rash claim anathematized by the Fathers that it is impossible for the rectified to keep

---

1. This appendix contains a translation of a few lines from the proemium of the Council's Decree on Rectification (*Decretum de Justificatione*), followed by the eleventh and thirteenth chapters of that Decree in their entirety, together with the eighteenth, twenty-second, and twenty-fifth canons. These are the conciliar texts of most importance to Pascal in the *Writings*. I translate from the Latin given in Tanner, 2:671, 675–76, 680. The source notes provided here are the same as those given in Tanner. I have consulted with profit the English translation given in Tanner, as well as that in Denzinger, §§1520, 1536–1539, 1541, 1568, 1572, 1575; but neither seems to me altogether satisfactory.

2. Malachi 3:20.

3. Hebrews 12:2.

God's precepts. For God does not command impossibilities, but by commanding something, warns that we should do what we can and entreat for what we cannot, and he provides help so that we can;[4] for his commandments are not heavy,[5] but his yoke is easy and his burden light.[6] For those who are God's children love Christ; and those who love him (as he testified himself) keep his words,[7] which they are able to do with divine help.

In this mortal life, it is inevitable that people, however holy and righteous, sometimes fall into sin, at least into those light and everyday sins called venial. They do not thereby cease to be righteous—for the voice of the righteous that says "forgive us our sins"[8] is humble and true. So it is that the righteous ought all the more take themselves to be obliged to walk in the way of righteousness, because now that they are "freed from sin and become God's slaves,"[9] and are living "soberly and justly and piously,"[10] they are able to improve through Christ Jesus from whom they gained access to that grace.[11] For God does not desert those once rectified by his grace unless they first deserted him.[12]

Therefore, none should flatter themselves with faith alone, supposing themselves to have become heirs and to have gotten their inheritance by faith alone, without suffering with Christ so as to be glorified with him.[13] For Christ himself, (as the Apostle says), "though Son of God, learned obedience through what he suffered, and, being perfected, became the source of eternal salvation for all who obey him."[14] And so the Apostle himself warns the rectified, saying, "Do you not know that all the runners in a race compete, but one wins the prize? Run so that you will win. I run in that way; I do not fight uselessly, like

4. Augustine, *De natura* 43.50.

5. 1 John 5:3.

6. Matthew 11:30.

7. John 14:23.

8. Matthew 6:12.

9. Romans 6:22.

10. Titus 2:12.

11. Romans 5:2.

12. Augustine, *De natura* 26.29.

13. Romans 8:17.

14. Hebrews 5:8–9.

someone punching the air, but I chastise my body, reducing it to slavery so that, after preaching to others, I might not myself be disqualified."[15] And Peter, the prince of apostles: "Be zealous, so that you might confirm through your good works your call and your election. In doing this, you will never sin."[16] From which it is clear that those who say that the righteous sin at least venially in every good work,[17] or (yet more intolerable) that they deserve eternal punishment, oppose orthodox religious doctrine. Similarly, those who hold that the righteous sin in everything they do if, when arousing themselves from torpor and encouraging themselves to run the race, as well as glorifying God above all, they also look for eternal reward, since it is written, "I have turned my heart toward doing your statutes for the sake of reward,"[18] and the Apostle said of Moses that he looked for reward.[19]

Chapter XIII: On the Gift of Perseverance

Similarly with respect to the gift of perseverance, about which it is written: "Those who persevere to the end will be saved."[20] (Which can come from nowhere else than the one who has the power to keep standing those who stand,[21] so that they might persevere in standing, and to lift up those who fall.) For none should promise themselves any outcome with absolute certainty, but rather all should place their firmest hope in God's help, and should rest there. For unless they themselves turn against his grace, God will bring the good work to completion as he began it,[22] working both the will and the performance.[23]

Nonetheless, those who take themselves to stand should take care that they do not fall,[24] and should with fear and trembling work for

15. 1 Corinthians 9:24, 26–27.

16. 2 Peter 1:10.

17. *Exsurge Domini* 31–32; Denzinger §§1481–1482.

18. Psalm 119:112.

19. Hebrews 11:26.

20. Matthew 10:22, 24:13.

21. Romans 14:4.

22. Philippians 1:6.

23. Philippians 2:13.

24. 1 Corinthians 10:12.

their own salvation[25] with efforts, and vigils, and almsgiving, and prayer, and offerings, and fasting, and chastity.[26] For knowing themselves to be reborn to the hope of glory,[27] and not yet to glory, they ought fear the combat with the world, the flesh, and the Devil, which they cannot win unless, with the grace of God ,they obey what the Apostle says. "We are not in thrall to the flesh so that we should live according to it, for if you live according to the flesh, you will die. But if you put the actions of the flesh to death by way of the spirit, you will live."[28]

Canon Eighteen

Any who say that God's precepts cannot be kept even by those rectified and under grace are to be anathematized.

Canon Twenty-Two

Any who say that the rectified can persevere in the righteousness they have received without God's particular help, or cannot do so with that help, are to be anathematized.

Canon Twenty-Five

Any who say that the righteous sin at least venially in whatever good works they do or, (what is more intolerable), sin mortally and therefore deserve eternal punishments and are not damned only because God does not impute those works to their damnation, are to be anathematized.

25. Philippians 2:12.
26. 2 Corinthians 6:5–6.
27. 1 Peter 1:3.
28. Romans 8:12–13.

BIBLIOGRAPHY

This list contains all the works mentioned in this book, as well as a selection of others consulted in preparing it. It is comprehensive neither as to secondary sources on the *Writings*, nor as to those used by Pascal in his composition of them. All Pascal's principal sources are, however, identified, and for those I provide, in addition to bibliographic information, a brief comment on the nature of their presence in the *Writings*.

It was commonplace in the sixteenth and seventeenth centuries to publish pseudonymously or anonymously, and many of the works from that period in this list were so published. I follow scholarly consensus, when there is one, in giving the true names of the authors or compilers of these works. I modernize the spelling and capitalization of sixteenth- and seventeenth-century French titles, and sometimes abbreviate them, indicated by [&c]. An indication that a section of a premodern work (e.g., *De civitate Dei* 14.11) is deployed by Pascal neither implies nor rules out his use of the entire section; it guarantees only that he quotes, alludes to, or echoes some part of it. References to one or another of the *Writings* in this bibliography are by number—e.g., §1.

Alcantara, Jean-Pascal. "Pascal et Calvin." In *Pascal*, edited by Dominique Descotes, 113–42.

Arnauld, Antoine. *Apologie de Monsieur Jansénius eveque d'Ypre & de la doctrine de S. Augustin, expliquée dans son livre, intitulé* Augustinus [&c]. Paris, 1644.

Pascal does not mention this in the *Writings*, but it is a presence behind much therein, especially its chronological arrangement of pro-Augustinian sources on grace at 293–345. Pascal draws from this for his discussion in §15 of the various condemnations of the new (Molinist) theologians in France in the late sixteenth and early seventeenth centuries.

————. *Apologie pour les saints Pères de l'Église, défenseurs de la grâce de Jésus-Christ* [&c]. Paris, 1651.

Used by Pascal for his discussion in §15 of the censures provided by the theological faculties of Douai and Louvain; and possibly for some of the citations of Aquinas in §§1, 5, 15.

————. *Seconde lettre de Monsieur Arnauld, docteur de Sorbonne, à un duc et pair de France.* Second edition. Paris, 1655.

Pascal had clearly read this, and it may be the source of his mentions of and quotations from the Second Council of Orange and the Third Council of Valence in §2 and §14.

Augustine. *Ad Simplicianum.*

Pascal deploys 1.2.12 (§5); and 1.2.21 (§13).

————. *Contra Adimantum Manichaei discipulum.*

Pascal deploys 26.1 (§§1, 5, 9, 12).

————. *Contra duas epistulas Pelagianorum.*

Pascal deploys 1.2.4 (§2); 1.2.5 (§§2, 14); 1.3.6 (§13); 1.3.7 (§13); 1.15.29 (§§2, 14); 2.9.19 (§5) and 2.9.21 (§13).

————. *Contra Julianum.*

Pascal deploys 4.3.18 (§13); and 4.8.42 (§1).

————. *Contra Julianum opus imperfectum.*

Pascal deploys 1.6 (§§2, 14); 1.75 (§§2, 14); 1.94 (§13); 1.96 (§§2, 14); 1.97 (§§2, 14); 1.108 (§5); 1.109 (§§5, 13); 1.115 (§§2, 14); and 2.157 (§5).

————. *De civitate Dei.*

Pascal deploys 14.11 and 21.16 (§13).

————. *De correptione et gratia.*

Pascal deploys 3.5 (§10); 7.11 (§5); 12.34 (§8); 13.40 (§6); 13.41 (§1); and 13.42 (§§8, 9, 12).

————. *De dono perseverantiae.*

Pascal deploys 6.10 (§12); 7.13 (§§8, 9); and 23.64 (§§8, 9).

————. *De Genesi adversus Manicheos.*

Pascal deploys 1.3.6 (§§9, 12).

————. *De gratia Christi et de peccato originali.*

Pascal deploys 1.13.14 (§13); 1.14.15 (§5); and 1.31.33 (§§2, 14).

———. *De gratia et libero arbitrio.*
Pascal deploys 8.20–9.21 (§1); 15.31 (§§1, 9); 16.32 (§§2, 10, 12); and 17.33 (§9).

———. *De natura et gratia.*
Pascal deploys 18.20 (§15); 26.29 (§5); 42.49–43.50 (§§1, 14); and 69.83 (§§1, 9, 10, 14, 15).

———. *De nuptiis et concupiscentia.*
Pascal deploys 2.3.8 (§§2, 14).

———. *De peccatorum meritis et remissione et de baptismo parvulorum.*
Pascal deploys 2.3.3 (§§2, 14); 2.6.7 (§14); 2.8.19 (§6); 2.17.26 (§13); 2.17.27 (§§6, 9, 13); 2.19.33 (§§6, 9, 13).

———. *De perfectione justitiae hominis.*
Pascal deploys 5.11 (§10); 10.21 (§§1, 10, 14); and 10.22 (§10).

———. *De praedestinatione sanctorum.*
Pascal deploys 3.7 (§5); 7.12 (§1); and 8.13 (§5).

———. *De spiritu et littera.*
Pascal deploys 3.5 (§13); 30.52 (§§2, 14); and 35.63 (§§13).

———. *Enarrationes in Psalmos.*
Pascal deploys 118.14.2 (§§8, 9).

———. *Enchiridion.*
Pascal deploys 9.30 (§13); 9.31 (§5); 22.81 (§§5, 13); 31.118 (§13); and 32.121 (§§9, 12).

———. *Epistulae.*
Pascal deploys 145.4 (§13); 157.2.10 (§§2, 14); 194.4.16 (§§8, 9); 217.4.14 (§6); 217.5.16 (§1); and 217.6.19 (§1).

———. *Expositio epistulae ad Galatas.*
Pascal deploys 49 (§8).

———. *In epistulam Johannis ad Parthos tractatus.*
Pascal deploys 4.6 (§1).

———. *In Johannis evangelium tractatus.*
Pascal deploys 26.4 (§13).

———. *Opera D. Aurelii Augustini Hipponensis episcopi et doctoris praecipui* [&c]. 10 books in 6 vols. Antwerp: Christopher Plantin, 1576–1577.
Pascal certainly knew and used this edition, but the evidence of his doing so in the *Writings* is limited, probably, to three of the Latin excerpts in §14.

———. *Retractationes.*

Pascal deploys 1.10.2 (§§5, 9, 12); and 1.22.4 (§§1, 5, 9, 12).

———. *Sermones.*

Pascal deploys 15.11 (§12); 156.12.13 (§1); 156.9.9 (§13); and 169.11.13 (§§7, 12).

Bossut, Charles, ed. *Oeuvres de Blaise Pascal.* 5 vols. The Hague: Detune, 1779.

Bourzeis, Amable de. *Lettre d'un Abbé à un Président sur la conformité de saint Augustin avec le Concile de Trente, touchant la manière dont les justes peuvent délaisser Dieu et être ensuite délaissés de lui.* 1649.

This is mentioned by Pascal in §9, and used there and elsewhere for his analysis of the double desertion.

———. *Propositiones de gratia in Sorbonae Facultate propediem examinandae.* 1649.

This was certainly known to Pascal, and probably among his sources for his citations of and quotations from Prosper's *De gratia Dei et libero arbitrio contra Collatorem*, and perhaps for some texts from Aquinas's *Summa Theologiae*.

———. *Saint Augustin victorieux de Calvin et de Molina ou Réfutation d'un livre intitulé* Le Secret du Jansenisme [&c]. Paris, 1652.

Pascal's principal source for his depictions of Calvinism and Molinism.

Briggs, Robin. "The Gallican Context for Pascal's Writings on Grace." *Seventeenth-Century French Studies* 35, no. 2 (2013): 125–35.

Brunschvicg, Léon, Pierre Boutroux, & Félix Gazier. Eds. *Oeuvres de Blaise Pascal, suivante l'ordre chronologique.* Vol. 11. Paris: Hachette, 1914.

Cantillon, Alain. "Blaise Pascal ou la séparation béante." *Archives de sciences sociales des religions* 59, no. 166 (2014): 35–45.

———. "Mais comment donc écrire sur la Grâce?" *Seventeenth-Century French Studies* 35, no. 2 (2013): 116–24.

Carraud, Vincent. "Subtilité et supposition métaphysiques dans la *Lettre sur la possibilité des commandements.*" *Quaderni Leif* 9, no. 13 (2015): 7–21.

Censurae Facultatum Sacrae Theologiae Lovaniensis ac Duacensis. Paris, 1641.

Pascal draws his quotations from this in §15 principally, and perhaps exclusively, from Arnauld, *Jansénius*, 332–40.

Chevalier, Jacques, ed. *Pascal: Oeuvres complètes.* Paris: Gallimard, 1954.

Chifflet, Philip, ed. *Sacrosancti et Oecumenici Concilii Tridentini Paulo III, Iulio III, et Pio IV, Pontificibus Maximis Celebrati Canones et Decreta.* Antwerp: Balthasar Moretus, 1640.

Pascal's principal source for the Council of Trent's Decree on Rectification.

Claudel, Paul. *Oeuvres complètes*. 3 vols. Paris: Gallimard, 1950.

Compagnon, Antoine. *Un été avec Pascal*. Paris: Équateurs-Humensis / France Inter, 2020.

Conrius, Florent. *Peregrinus Jerichuntinus, hoc est, de natura humana feliciter instituta, infeliciter lapsa, miserabiliter vulnerata, misericorditer restaurata*. Paris: Claude Calleville, 1641.

This is mentioned by Pascal in §15. He may have consulted it in its original Latin, as cited, or in a French rendering by Arnauld: *Abrégé de la doctrine de saint Augustin touchant la grâce* (1645).

Council of Trent. *Decretum et Canones De justificatione*.

Pascal frequently quotes, mentions, draws from, and analyzes the eleventh and thirteenth chapters of the Decree, together with the eighteenth, twenty second, and twenty-fifth canons. His most extended discussions are in §§1, 3, 4, 5. He draws his texts exclusively from Chifflet.

de La Bigne, Marguerin, ed. *Bibliothecae Veterum Patrum seu Auctorum Ecclesiasticorum* [&c]. 4 vols. Paris, 1624.

Denzinger, Heinrich. *Enchiridion Symbolorum Definitionum et Declarationum de Rebus Fidei et Morum*. Forty-third bilingual (Latin/English) edition. Edited by Peter Hünermann, Robert Fastiggi, and Anne Englund Nash. San Francisco: Ignatius Press, 2012.

Descotes, Dominique. *L'Argumentation chez Pascal*. Paris: Presses Universitaires de France, 1993.

———. "Le raisonnement par l'absurde dans les *Écrits sur la grâce*." In *Pascal*, edited by Dominique Descotes, 393–432.

———. "Pascal et Bourzeis." *Quaderni Leif* 9, no. 13 (2015): 23–47.

Descotes, Dominique, ed. *Pascal, auteur spirituel*. Paris: Honoré Champion, 2006.

Desmares, Toussaint-Guy-Joseph. *Réponse d'un docteur en théologie à Monsieur Chamillard, docteur et professeur de Sorbonne*. 1656.

Pascal's source for Estius's commentary on Lombard's *Sentences*, as quoted in §2.

Estius, Guillaume. *Sententiarum Commentarii in quatuor libros sententiarum Petri Lombardi*. Douai, 1616.

Pascal mentions this and in §2 quotes from 3.27.6, in both Latin and French.

Ferreyrolles, Gérard. "Les citations de saint Thomas dans les *Écrits sur la grâce*." In *Pascal*, edited by Dominique Descotes, 143–59.

Franceschi, Sylvio Hermann de. "Le moment pascalien dans la querelle de la grâce: Pascal à la croisée des chemins (1655–1657)." *Revue de Synthèse* 4 (2009): 595–635.

Frigo, Alberto. "État présent des études sur les *Écrits sur la grâce* (1991–2015)." *Quaderni Leif* 9, no. 13 (2015): 49–61.

Fulgentius of Ruspe. *Ad Monimum*.

Pascal deploys 1.9 (§1); and 2.14 (§9).

————. *De veritate praedestinationis et gratiae Dei.*

Pascal deploys 1.15.33–1.16.34 (§§8, 9); 1.18.38 (§8, 9); and 2.4.6 (§§8, 9, 10).

————. *Epistulae.*

Pascal deploys 4.2 (§9); and 6.6 (§8).

Gouhier, Henri. *Blaise Pascal: Commentaires.* Paris: Vrin, 1966.
Griffiths, Paul J. *Why Read Pascal?* Washington, DC: The Catholic University of America Press, 2021.
Hammond, Nicholas. "Pascal's *Fragments d'un discours amoureux.*" *Seventeenth-Century French Studies* 35, no. 2 (2013): 169–78.
Jansenius, Cornelius. *Augustinus.* 3 vols. Louvain: Iacobus Zegenus, 1640.
Jerome. *Dialogus adversus Pelagianos.*

Pascal deploys 1.21–1.24 (§14).

————. *Epistulae.*

Pascal deploys 133.3–4 (*ad Ctesiphontem*) (§§2, 14); and 148.5 (*ad Celantem*, which may not be by Jerome) (§14).

————. *Epistolae D. Hieronymi, Stridoniensis, et Libri Contra Haereticos* [&c]. Antwerp: Christopher Plantin, 1578.

Pascal may have used this edition of Jerome for his quotations from Jerome's letters in §§2, 14.

Jovy, Ernest, ed. *Pascal inédit.* Paris: Tavernier, 1908.
Kambouchner, Denis. "Pascal et le temps de grâce." *Quaderni Leif* 9, no. 13 (2015): 63–75.
Kolakowski, Leszek. *Chrétiens sans Église: La conscience religieuse et le lien confessionel au XVIIe siècle.* Paris: Gallimard, 1969.
————. *God Owes Us Nothing: A Brief Remark on Pascal's Religion and on the Spirit of Jansenism.* Chicago: University of Chicago Press, 1995.
Krailsheimer, A. J., trans. *Pascal: The Provincial Letters.* Baltimore: Penguin Books, 1967.
Lafuma, Louis. *Pascal: Deux pièces imparfaites sur la Grâce et le Concile de Trente.* Paris: Vrin, 1948.
Lafuma, Louis, ed. *Pascal: Oeuvres complètes.* Paris: Éditions du Seuil, 1963.
Le Guern, Michel, ed. *Pascal: Oeuvres complètes.* 2 vols. Paris: Éditions Gallimard, 1998, 2000.
————. *Études sur la vie et les Pensées de Pascal.* Paris: Honoré Champion, 2015.
Lettieri, Gaetano. *Il metodo della grazia: Pascal e l'ermeneutica giansenista di Agostino.* Rome: Edizione Dehoniane, 1999.
Levi, Anthony and Honor Levi, eds. and trans. *Pascal: Pensées and Other Writings.* Oxford: Oxford University Press, 1995.
Mesnard, Jean. "Conclusions ou perspectives sur le mystère de la grâce." *Quaderni Leif* 9, no. 13 (2015): 141–56.
————. "Histoire secrète de la recherche pascalienne au XXe siècle." In *Pascal – New Trends in Port-Royal Studies*, edited by David Wetsel and Frédéric Canovas, 13–38. Tübingen: Gunter Narr, 2002.

———. *Pascal: l'homme et l'oeuvre*. Paris: Boivin, 1951.

Mesnard, Jean, ed. *Pascal: Oeuvres complètes*. 4 vols. (incomplete). Paris: Desclée de Brouwer, 1964–1991.

Miel, Jan. *Pascal and Theology*. Baltimore & London: Johns Hopkins University Press, 1969.

Migne, J.-P. *Patrologiae Cursus Completus, Series Latina*. Paris, 1844–1855 (with later reprints). Consulted via the portal at https://www.documenta catholicaomnia.eu/25_10_40-_Imagines.html at various dates between 2020 and 2023.

Mochizuki Yuka. "La délectation dans les *Écrits sur la grâce*. Une orientation nouvelle dans les controverses jansénistes." In *Pascal*, edited by Dominique Descotes, 351–92.

Moriarty, Michael. "Martin de Barcos: Grace, Predestination, and Jansenism." *Seventeenth-Century French Studies* 35, no. 2 (2013): 148–68.

———. "Pascal, Molina, et le molinisme." *Quaderni Leif* 9, no. 13 (2015): 77–90.

Parish, Richard. "État Présent: Blaise Pascal." *French Studies* 71, no. 4 (2017): 539–50.

———. "Preliminary Remarks on Pascal's Écrits sur la grâce." *Seventeenth-Century French Studies* 35, no. 2 (2013): 101–5.

———. "Relire les *Écrits sur la grâce* à la lumière des écrits sur la grâce: orthodoxie et esthétique." *Quaderni Leif* 9, no. 13 (2015): 91–102.

Pasqua, Hervé. *Blaise Pascal: Penseur de la grâce*. Paris: Téqui, 2000.

Pécharman, Martine. "Les Écrits sur la grâce ou de la bonne manière d'être augustinien." *Seventeenth-Century French Studies* 35, no. 2 (2013): 106–15.

———. *Pascal: Qu'est-ce que la vérité?* Paris: Presses Universitaires de France, 2000.

Pelagius. *Libellus fidei ad Innocentem Papam.*

Pascal deploys 6 (§§2, 14).

Pezzino, Giuseppe. "Conclusions, ou mieux une pause dans les travaux en cours." *Quaderni Leif* 9, no. 13 (2015): 157–60.

Prosper of Aquitaine. *Ad capitula objectionum Vincentianarum responsiones.*

Pascal deploys 14 (§§1, 8, 9, 12).

———. *Carmen de ingratis.*

Pascal perhaps indicates this in §2.

———. *De gratia Dei et libero arbitrio contra Collatorem.*

Pascal deploys 6 (§13), and may implicitly refer to 21 (§2).

———. *Epistula ad Demetriadem de vera humilitate.*

Pascal deploys 13 (§§2, 14); and 15 (§§10, 14).

———. *Epistula ad Rufinum de gratia et libero arbitrio.*

Pascal deploys 1 (§1); and 8 (§§2, 14).

———. *Responsiones ad capitula Gallorum.*

Pascal deploys 6 (§§2, 14).

Rabourdin, David. *Pascal: Foi et conversion.* Paris: Presses Universitaires de France, 2013.

Romeo, Maria Vita. "Liberté et félicité dans les *Écrits sur la grâce.*" *Quaderni Leif* 9, no. 13 (2015): 103–21.

Sacy, Isaac Le Maître de, trans. *Poème de S. Prosper contre les ingrats* [&c]. 2nd ed. Paris: Martin Durand, 1650.

The source of Pascal's mention of the third chapter of Prosper's *Epistula ad Rufinum* (§1); and of Prosper's epitaphs for Nestorianism, implicitly mentioned (§2).

Scholar, Richard. "Epilogue: Cooperations." *Seventeenth-Century French Studies* 35, no. 2 (2013): 179–86.

Second Council of Orange. *Canones.*

Pascal deploys the twenty-fifth canon (§§2, 14).

Sellier, Philippe. "Conclusions croisées." *Quaderni Leif* 9, no. 13 (2015): 161–63.

———. *Pascal et la liturgie.* Paris: Presses Universitaires de France, 1966.

———. *Pascal et Saint Augustin.* Paris: Albin Michel, 1995. First published 1970.

Sinnich, Jean. *Sanctorum Patrum de gratia Christi et libero arbitrio dimicantium Trias, Augustinus Hipponensis adversus Pelagium, Prosper Aquitanicus adversus Cassianum, Fulgentius Ruspensis adversus Faustum* [&c]. 1648.

The source of a large majority of Pascal's quotations from and references to Augustine, Prosper, and Fulgentius, throughout the *Writings.*

Stiker-Métral, Charles-Olivier. "La manière d'écrire de Pascal dans les *Écrits sur la grâce*: La théologie à l'usage des honnêtes gens?" In *Pascal,* edited by Dominique Descotes, 325–49.

Tanner, Norman P., ed. *Decrees of the Ecumenical Councils.* 2 vols. London/ Washington, DC: Sheed & Ward/Georgetown University Press, 1990.

Third Council of Valence. *Canones.* Pascal deploys the third canon (§§2, 14).

Thirouin, Laurent. "De la *facilité* des commandements." *Quaderni Leif* 9, no. 13 (2015): 123–39.

Thomas Aquinas. *Summa theologiae.*

Pascal deploys 1.23.5, corpus (§1); 1.23.6, ad 2 (§5); 1–2.10.4, ad 3 (§5); 1–2.106.3, corpus (§15); 1–2.109.9, sed contra & corpus (§§5, 8, 9); 2–2.2.5 ad 1 (§15); and 3.22.4, ad 2 (§15).

Tonneau, Olivier. "'Sur les fonts plus belle et plus lumineuse que la soleil': Analyse sacramentelle et sociologique de la grâce." *Seventeenth-Century French Studies* 35, no. 2 (2013): 136–47.

Wittgenstein, Ludwig. *Philosophische Untersuchungen / Philosophical Investigations.* Translated by G. E. M. Anscombe, P. M. S. Hacker, and Joachim Schulte. Revised fourth edition. Malden, Massachusetts: Wiley-Blackwell, 2009.

Wood, William. *Blaise Pascal on Duplicity, Sin, and the Fall: The Secret Instinct.* Oxford: Oxford University Press, 2013.

Also in the Early Modern Catholic Sources series

A Defense of Free Will against Luther:
Assertionis Lutheranae Confutatio, Article 26
St. John Fisher
Translated by Thomas P. Scheck

On the Moderation of Reason in Religious Matters
Lodovico Antonio Muratori
Translated by Ulrich L. Lehner

Jansenism: An International Anthology
Edited by Shaun Blanchard and Richard T. Yoder

Discourses on the State and Grandeurs of Jesus:
The Ineffable Union of the Deity with Humanity
Pierre De Bérulle
Translated by Lisa Richmond

A Defense of Catholic Religion:
The Necessity, Existence and Limits of an Infallible Church
Beda Mayr, OSB
Translated by Ulrich L. Lehner

Metaphysical Disputations III and IV:
On Being's Passions in General and Its Principles
and On Transcendental Unity in General
Francisco Suárez
Translated and annotated, with corrected Latin text,
by Shane Duarte

Metaphysical Disputation II:
On the Essential Concept or the Concept of Being
Francisco Suárez
Translated and annotated, with corrected Latin text,
by Shane Duarte

The Predestination of Humans and Angels:
Augustinus, Tome III, Book IX
Cornelius Jansen
Translated by Guido Stucco

The Catholic Enlightenment:
A Global Anthology
Edited by Ulrich L. Lehner and Shaun Blanchard

Metaphysical Disputation I:
On the Nature of First Philosophy or Metaphysics
Francisco Suárez
Translated and annotated, with corrected Latin text,
by Shane Duarte

On the Motive of the Incarnation
The Salmanticenses
(Discalced Carmelites of Salamanca)
Translated by Dylan Schrader